JOE BONAMASSA
DRIVING TOWARDS THE DAYLIGHT

This book was approved by Joe Bonamassa
Cover illustration by Dennis Friel
Transcribed by Jeff Jacobson and Paul Pappas

Cherry Lane Music Company
Director of Publications/Project Editor: Mark Phillips

ISBN 978-1-4768-7457-9

Visit our website at www.cherrylaneprint.com

JOE BONAMASSA

DRIVING TOWARDS THE DAYLIGHT

Photo by Rick Phipps

In May 2012 unstoppable blues-rock juggernaut Joe Bonamassa released his "lucky" 13th album, *Driving Towards the Daylight*, which made its chart debut at No. 1 on the Blues chart, making this Joe's eighth No. 1 Blues album. The album also debuted at No. 21 on the Top 200 chart and No. 3 on the Independent chart. In the UK it debuted at No. 2, a career-best, outranking 2011's *Dust Bowl*, which peaked at No. 12.

Driving Towards the Daylight was produced by Kevin "Caveman" Shirley (Black Crowes, Aerosmith, Led Zeppelin). This is Kevin and Joe's seventh collaboration in six years. To support the release, Bonamassa's label, J&R Adventures, aired ten episodes of the reality miniseries *Driving Towards the Daylight*, which features three to four minute "webisodes," with interviews and footage of Joe and his band, as well as behind-the-scenes footage of the band recording *Driving Towards the Daylight* in the studio. The series can be viewed on Joe's YouTube channel: www.youtube.com/JoeBonamassaTV.

Recorded at Studio at the Palms in Las Vegas, the Village Recorder in Los Angeles, and the Cave in Malibu, *Driving Towards the Daylight* is a balanced back-to-basics album that highlights Bonamassa's signature style of roots blues with rock-and-roll guts while honoring the traditions of the original blues musicians. "We've taken some really traditional old blues songs—Howlin' Wolf's 'Who's Been Talking' and Robert Johnson's 'Stones in My Passway,' and we tried to imagine how they would have done them them in a rock context," said Shirley. "It's a very exciting return to the blues in a very visceral way. It's vibrant and it's gutsy and it's really, really rugged."

A unique group of musicians was gathered to record the album, including Aerosmith guitarist Brad Whitford (guitar), Blondie Chaplan (guitar), Anton Fig (drums and percussion), Arlan Schierbaum (keyboard), Michael Rhodes (bass), Carmine Rojas (bass), Jeff Bova and the Bovaland Brass, Pat Thrall (guitar), and Brad's son Harrison Whitford (guitar).

Throughout Joe's 21 years of performing professionally, he has had the honor of recording and sharing the stage with B.B. King, Eric Clapton, Peter Frampton, David Crosby, George Thorogood, Lynyrd Skynyrd, Jethro Tull, Ian Anderson, Glenn Hughes, Leslie West, Eric Johnson, Vince Gill, Tom Dowd, Phil Ramone, Jason Bonham, Jack Bruce, Ozzy Osbourne, Will Jennings, Warren Haynes, Motörhead, Tesla, Ted Nugent, Lemmy, and others. In April 2012 Bonamassa had the honor of playing—along with Billy Gibbons (ZZ Top) and Derek Trucks—at the Rock and Roll Hall of Fame induction of blues legend Freddie King.

DISLOCATED BOY

Words and Music by
Joe Bonamassa

*Gtrs. 1, 2 & 3: Open B tuning:
(tuned down, low to high) B-F♯-B-D♯-F♯-B

Intro
Moderately slow ♩ = 80

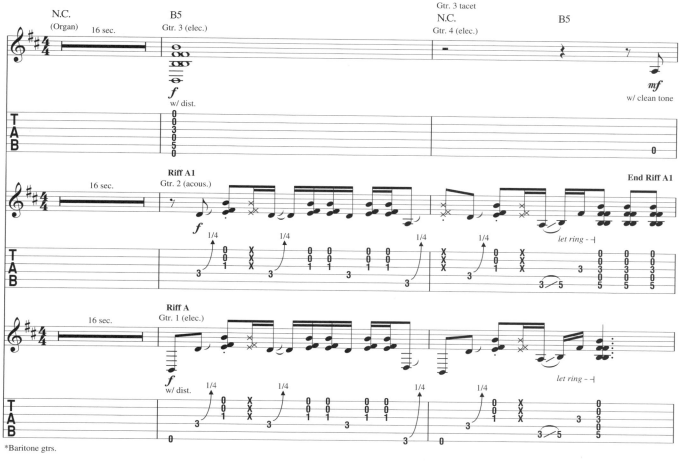

*Baritone gtrs.

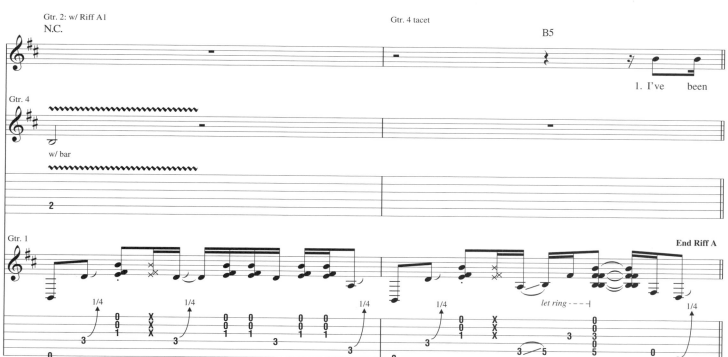

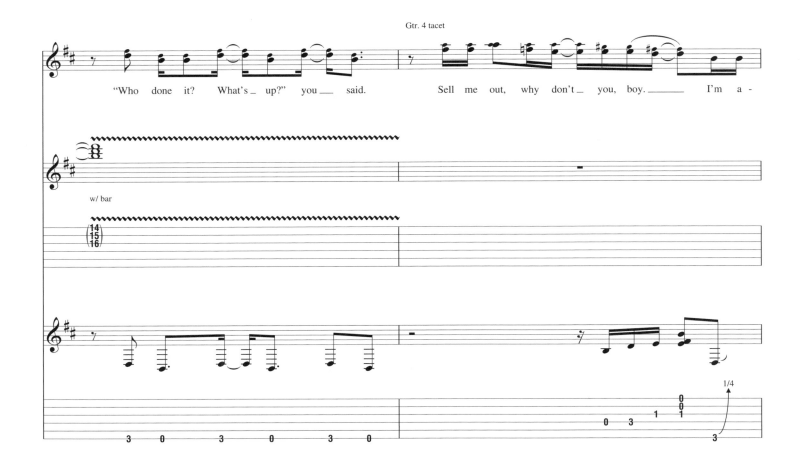

"Who done it? What's up?" you said. Sell me out, why don't you, boy. I'm a-

lone, severe-ly bro-ken; I'm a dis-lo-cat-ed boy.

Gtr. 2

Gtr. 1

End Riff B

Interlude

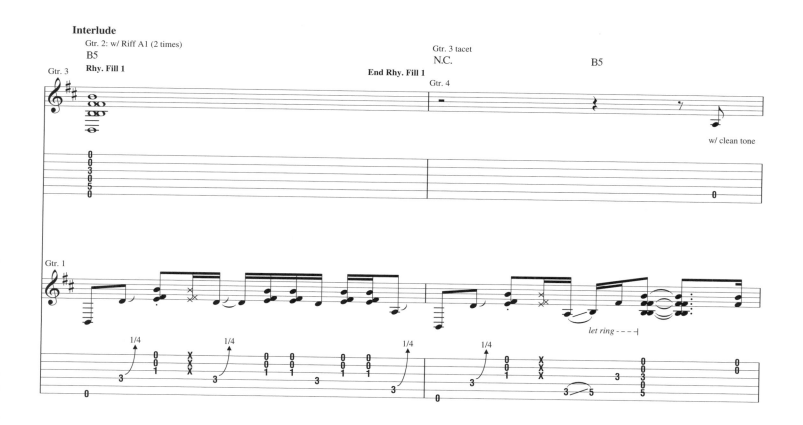

7

9

Chorus
Gtr. 1: w/ Riff B (1st 6 meas.)
Gtr. 2: w/ Riff A1 (3 times)

It's all ___ been for ___ you, ___ ba — by; I'm gon-na make it back ___ some-day. And I said,

hey now, knocked ___ down, why'd ___ you do it? Roll ___ me like ___ a hur-ri-cane.

All ___ is a bust ___ and I'm ___ numb like no — vo — caine. ___

"Who done it? What's ___ up?" you ___ said. Sell me out, why don't ___ you, boy. _____ I'm a-

Gtr. 2: w/ Riff D

lone, _____ se — vere — ly bro — ken; I'm a dis — lo — cat — ed boy. ___

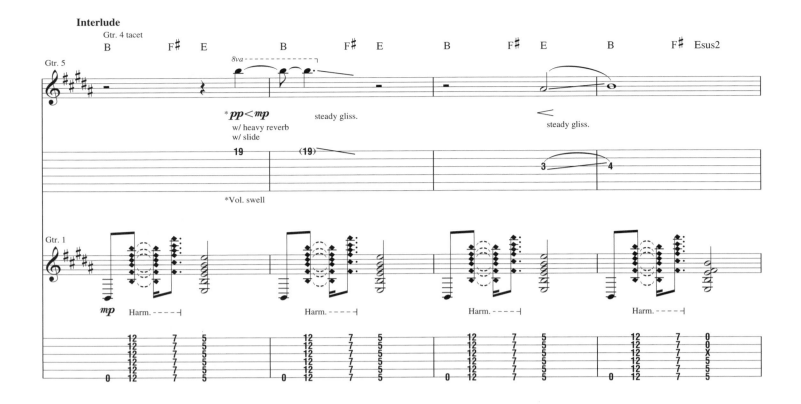

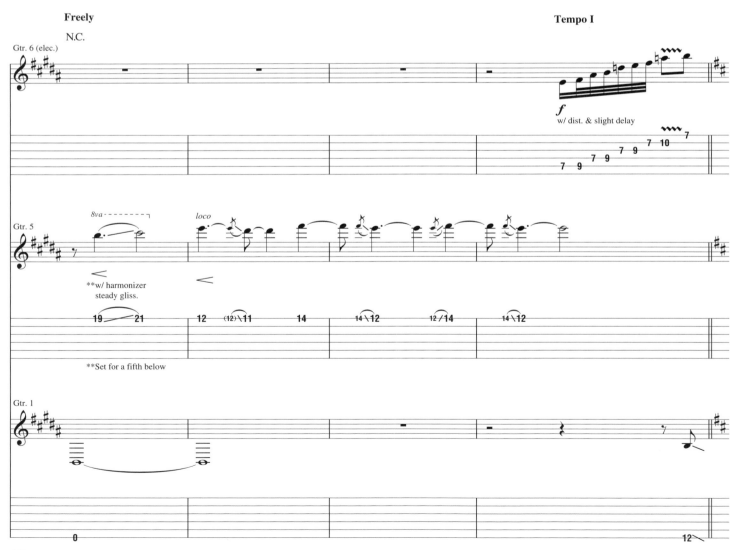

Guitar Solo

Gtr. 1: w/ Riff A (2 times)
Gtr. 2: w/ Riff A1 (4 times)
Gtr. 5 tacet

*Played behind the beat.

**As before

D.S. al Coda

4. So

Coda

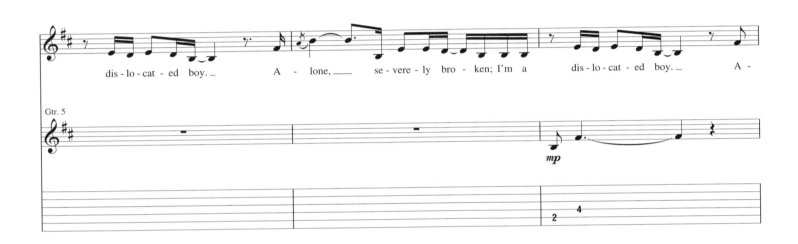

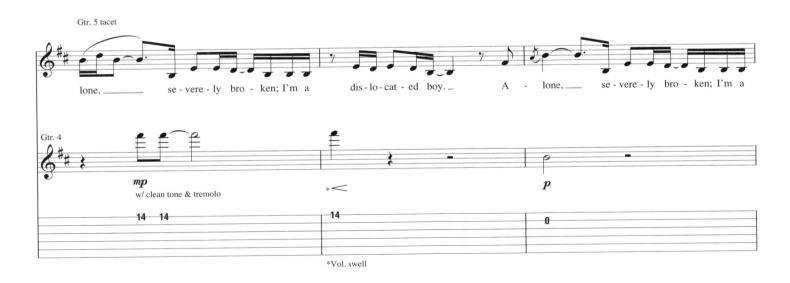

Outro-Guitar Solo
Gtr. 1: w/ Riff A (2 3/4 times)
Gtr. 2: w/ Riff A1 (5 1/2 times)
N.C.

lone, ___ se - vere - ly bro - ken; I'm a dis - lo - cat - ed boy. ___

*Catch and bend both strings
w/ ring finger till end of next meas.

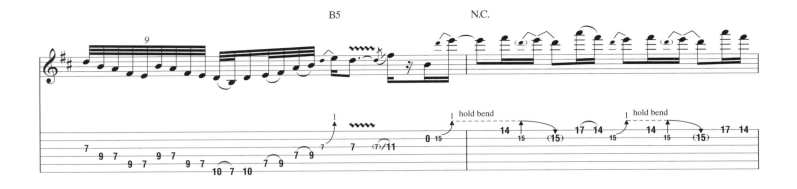

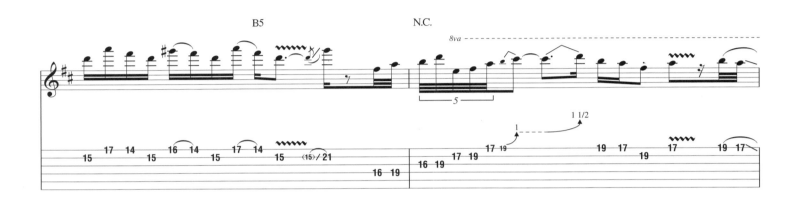

Free time

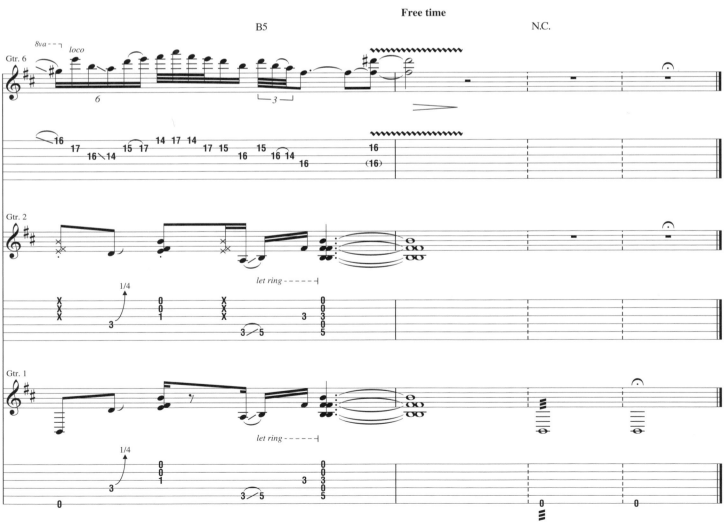

STONES IN MY PASSWAY

Words and Music by
Robert Johnson

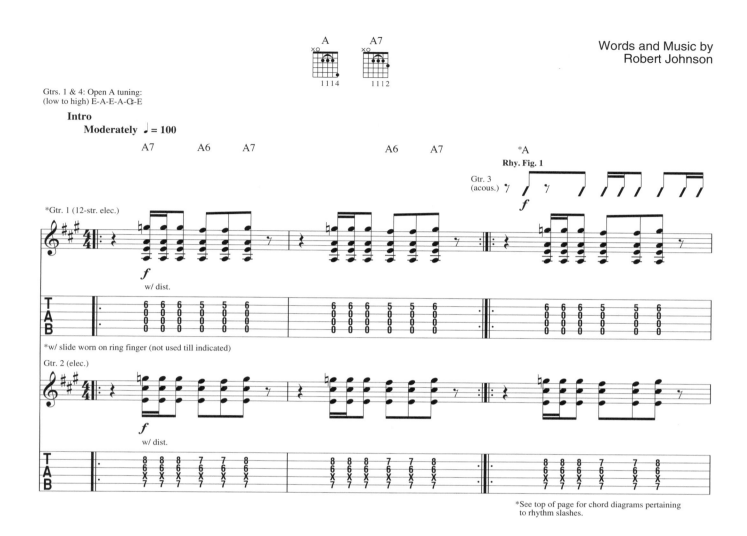

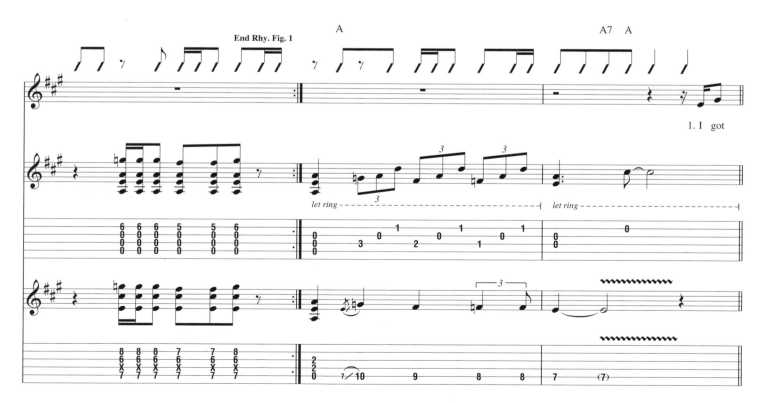

Verse

stones in my __ pass - way, __ and my road __ seems dark as night. __

w/ slide

let ring - - - - - -|

w/o slide

Rhy. Fig. 2

I got stones in my ___ pass - way, __ and my road __ seems dark as night. _

let ring -|

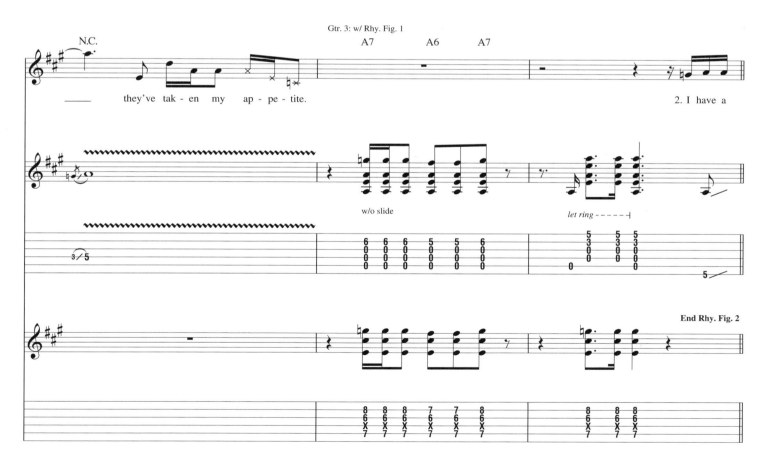

Verse

en - e - mies __ be - trayed __ me, __ have __ o - ver - tak - en poor __ Bob at last.

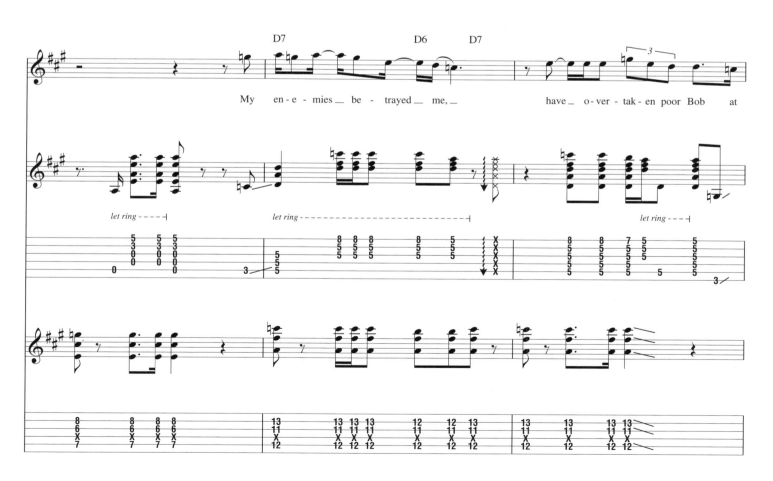

My en - e - mies __ be - trayed __ me, __ have __ o - ver - tak - en poor Bob at

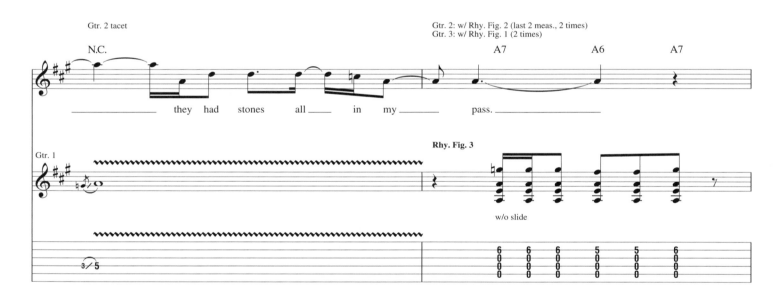

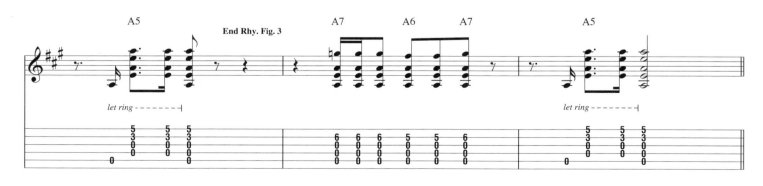

Guitar Solo

Gtr. 1 tacet

A7

Gtr. 4 (elec.)

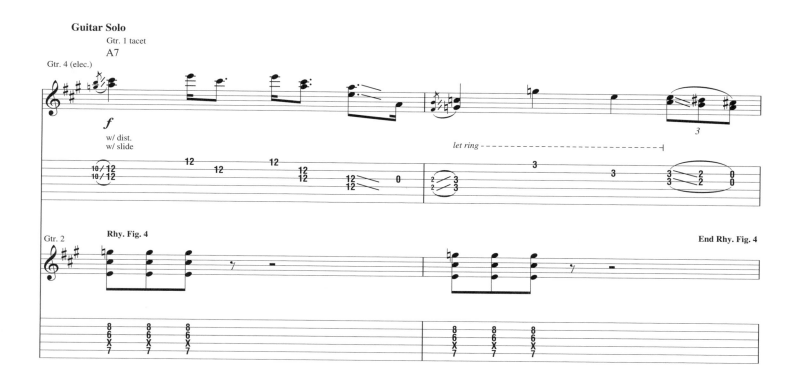

Gtr. 2: w/ Rhy. Fig. 4 (3 times)

Gtr. 4

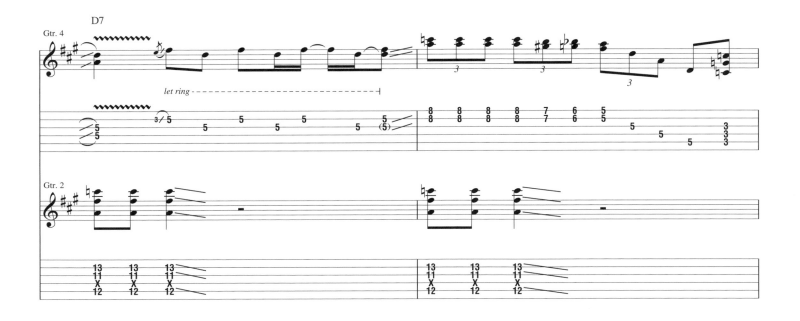

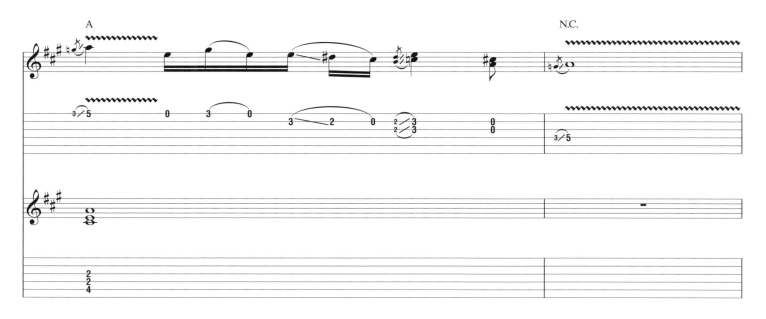

Gtr. 1: w/ Rhy. Fig. 3 (2 times)
Gtr. 2: w/ Rhy. Fig. 2 (last 2 meas., 2 times)
Gtr. 3: w/ Rhy. Fig. 1 (2 times)
Gtr. 4 tacet

4. Now, you

Verse

try'n' to take my life ___ and all my lov-in' too. ___ You laid a pass-way for me; now ___

Gtr. 1

w/ slide

Gtr. 2

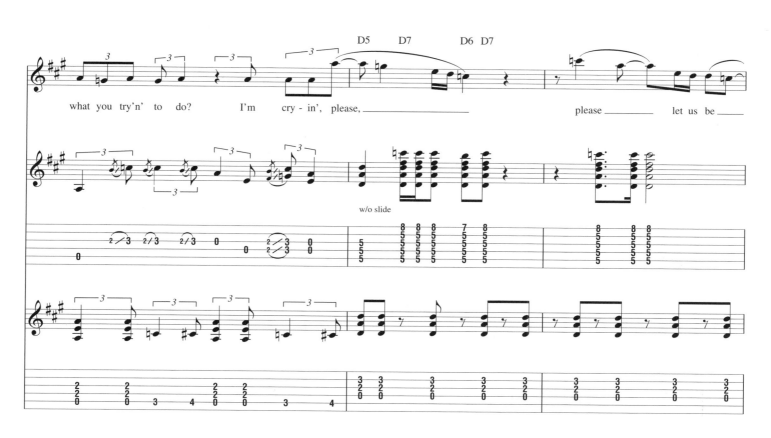

what you try'n' to do? I'm cry-in', please, ___ please ___ let us be ___

w/o slide

25

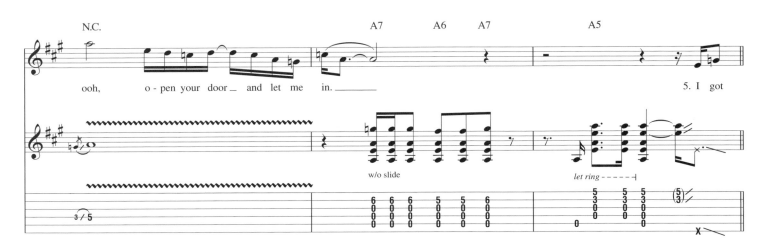

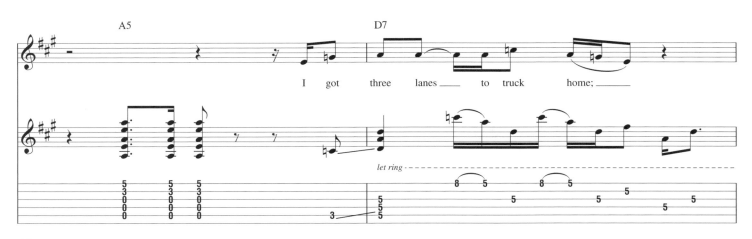

boys,   please   don't   block __ my   road. ____

I've   been   feel-in'   a-shamed   'bout   my   rid-er, _____   babe; __

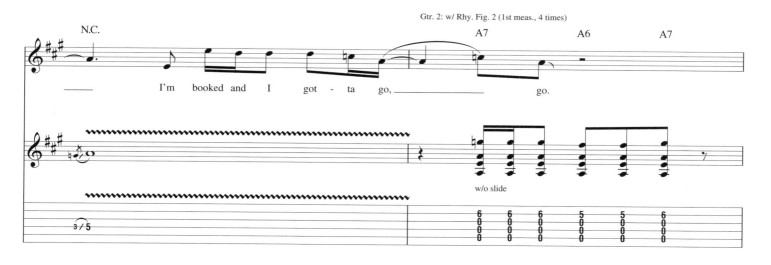

__   I'm   booked   and   I   got-ta   go, _____   go.

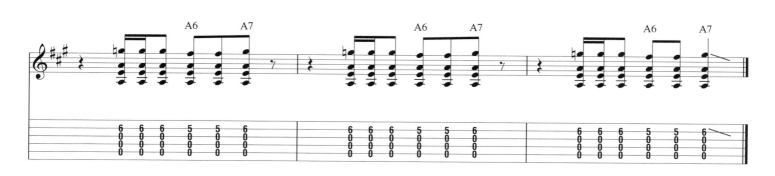

DRIVING TOWARDS THE DAYLIGHT

Words and Music by
Joe Bonamassa and Danny Kortchmar

Gtrs. 1, 3 & 4: Capo I

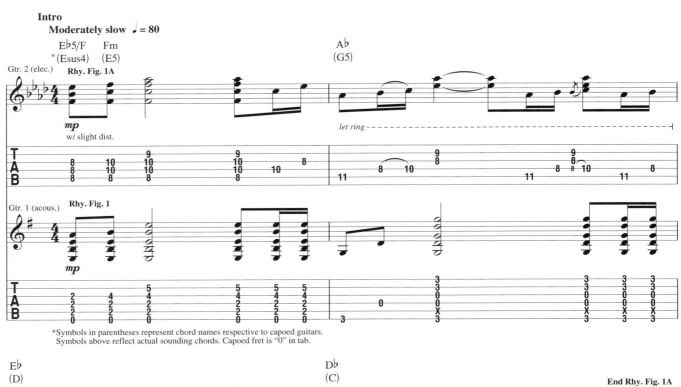

*Symbols in parentheses represent chord names respective to capoed guitars.
Symbols above reflect actual sounding chords. Capoed fret is "0" in tab.

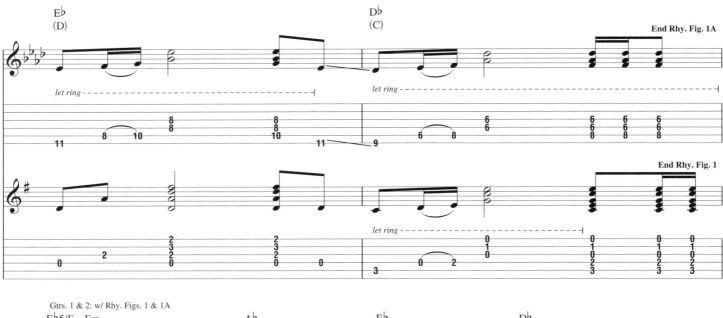

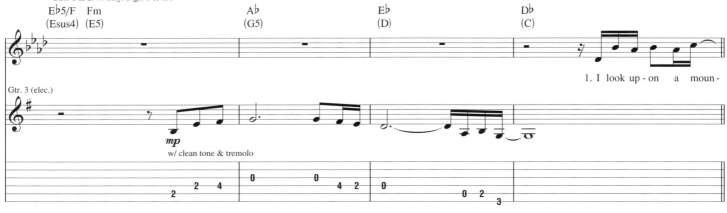

Verse

Gtr. 1: w/ Rhy. Fig. 1 (4 times)
Gtr. 2: w/ Rhy. Fig. 1A (2 3/4 times)

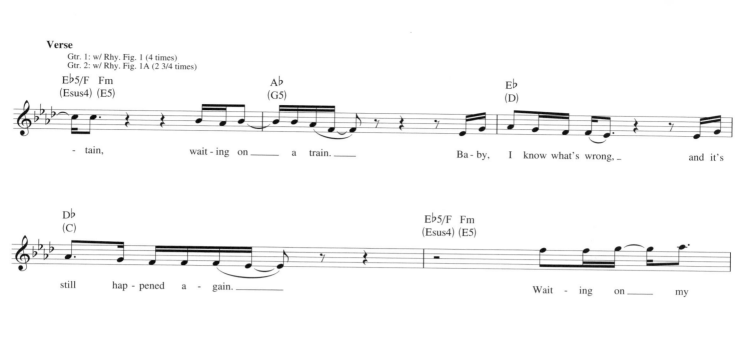

- tain,   wait - ing on ___ a train. ___   Ba - by,   I   know what's wrong, _   and it's

still   hap - pened a - gain. ___   Wait - ing   on ___   my

des - ti - ny, ___   learn - ing from   my ___   a - bil - i - ties. ___

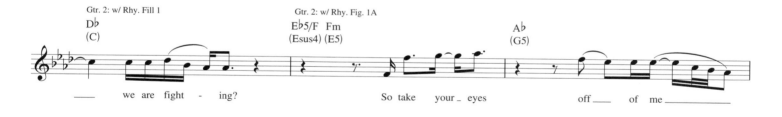

Who   was   wrong? _ And   who ___   was   right? _ And   do ___ we   e - ven   know   why _

Gtr. 2: w/ Rhy. Fill 1   Gtr. 2: w/ Rhy. Fig. 1A

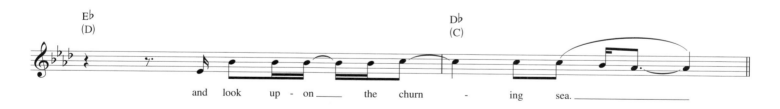

___   we are   fight - ing?   So   take   your _ eyes   off ___   of   me ___

and   look   up - on ___   the   churn   -   ing   sea. ___

29

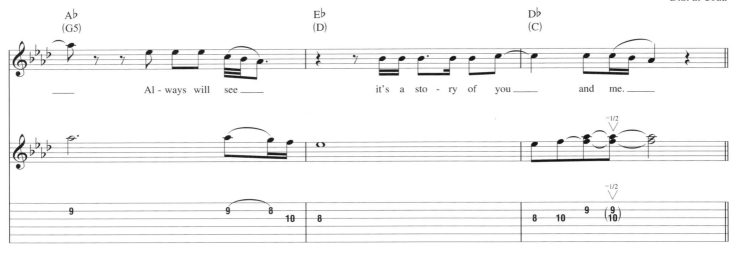

Al - ways will see _____ it's a sto - ry of you _____ and me. _____

⊕ Coda

Interlude

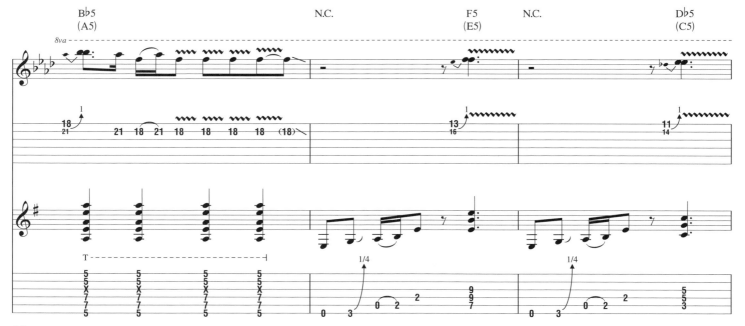

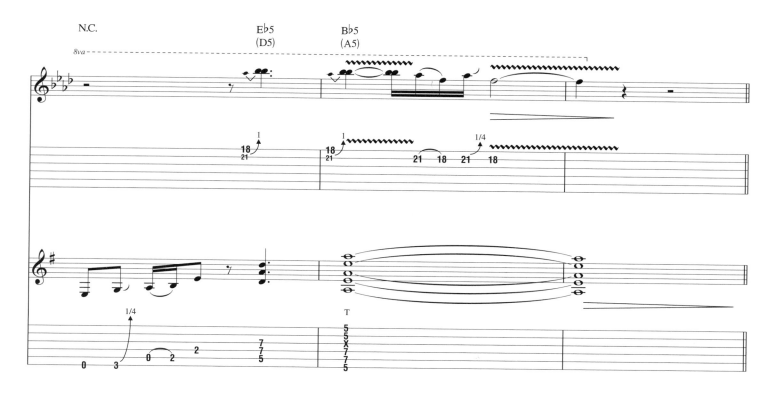

Breakdown-Chorus

Gtr. 1: w/ Rhy. Fig. 1 (2 times)
Gtrs. 4 & 6 tacet

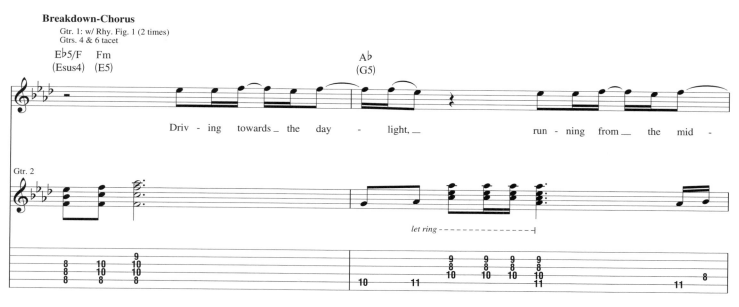

Driv-ing towards the day-light, run-ning from the mid-

let ring

-night, try'n' to get my way home. Run-ning from the spot-

let ring

- light, _ try'n' to find _ the day - light, _ try'n' to get _ my way _ home. _

let ring -------------------- let ring -------------------- let ring --------------------

Chorus

Gtrs. 1 & 2: w/ Rhy. Figs. 1 & 1A (2 times)
Gtr. 4: w/ Rhy. Fig. 2 (2 times)

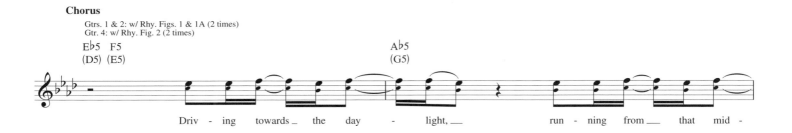

Eb5 F5   Ab5
(D5) (E5)   (G5)

Driv - ing towards _ the day - light, _ run - ning from _ that mid -

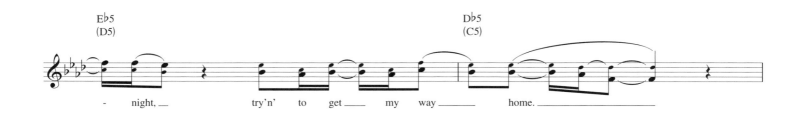

Eb5   Db5
(D5)   (C5)

- night, _ try'n' to get _ my way _ home. _

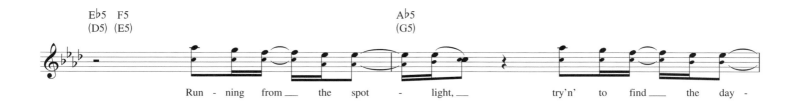

Eb5 F5   Ab5
(D5) (E5)   (G5)

Run - ning from _ the spot - light, _ try'n' to find _ the day -

Eb5   Db5
(D5)   (C5)

- light, _ try'n' to get _ my way _ home. _

Outro

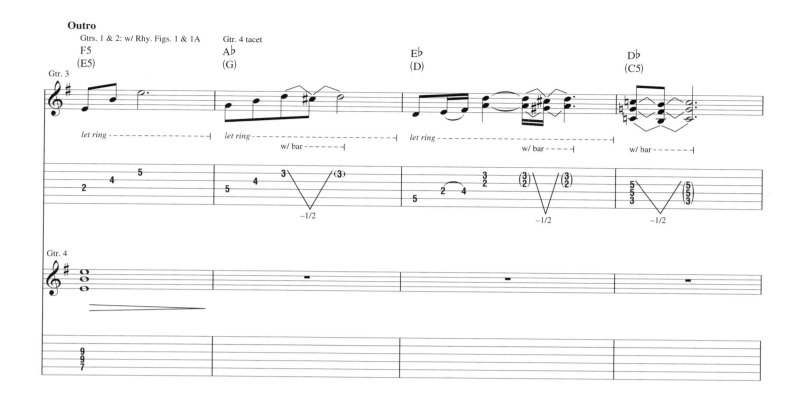

WHO'S BEEN TALKING?

Words and Music by
Chester Burnett

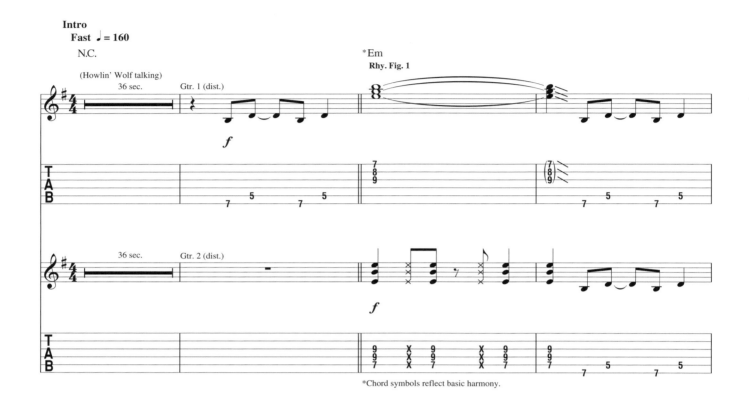

*Chord symbols reflect basic harmony.

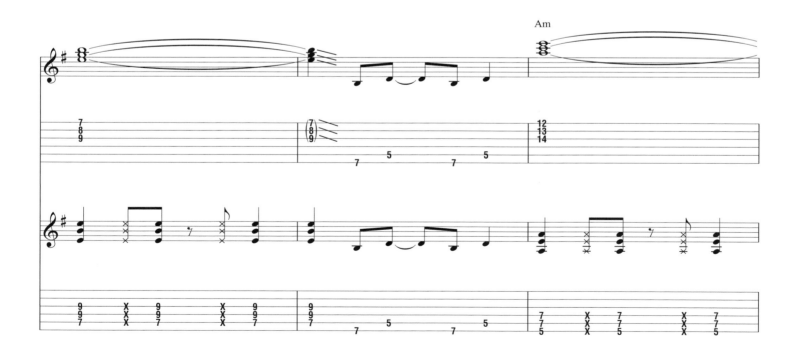

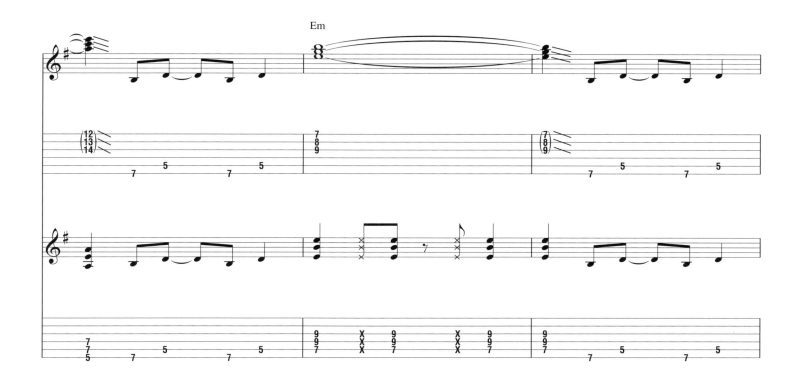

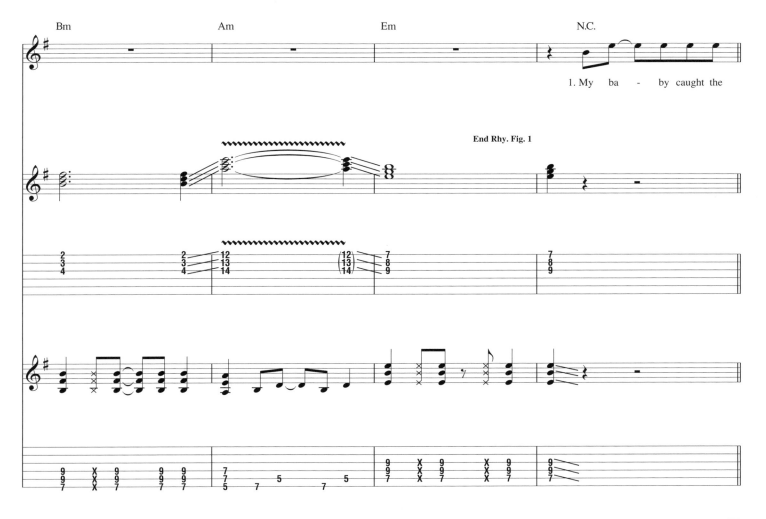

Verse

Gtr. 2: w/ Rhy. Fig. 2

tick - et,
ba - by,

long as her right arm.
hate to see you go.

My ba — by bought the
Well, good — bye,

Gtr. 1

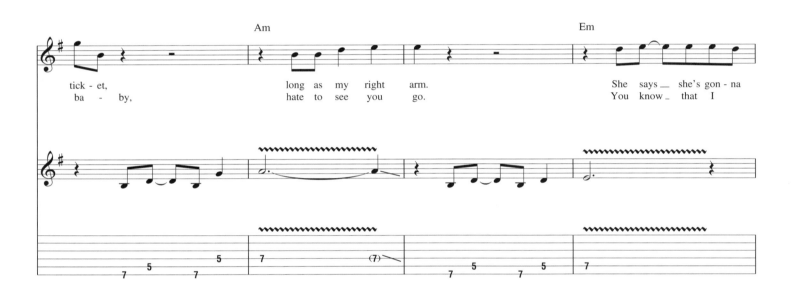

tick - et,
ba - by,

long as my right arm.
hate to see you go.

She says __ she's gon - na
You know __ that I

To Coda ⊕

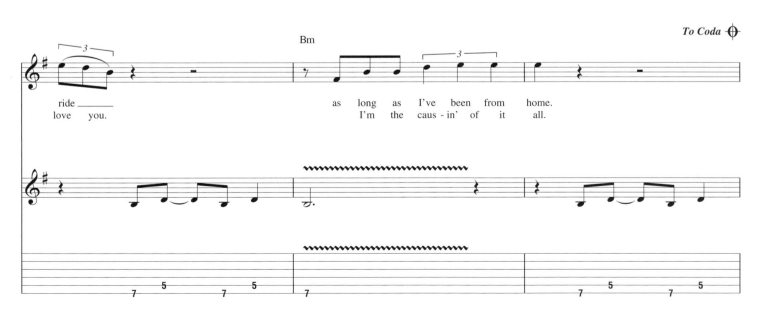

ride _____
love you.

as long as I've been from home.
I'm the caus - in' of it all.

40

3. Well, who's been

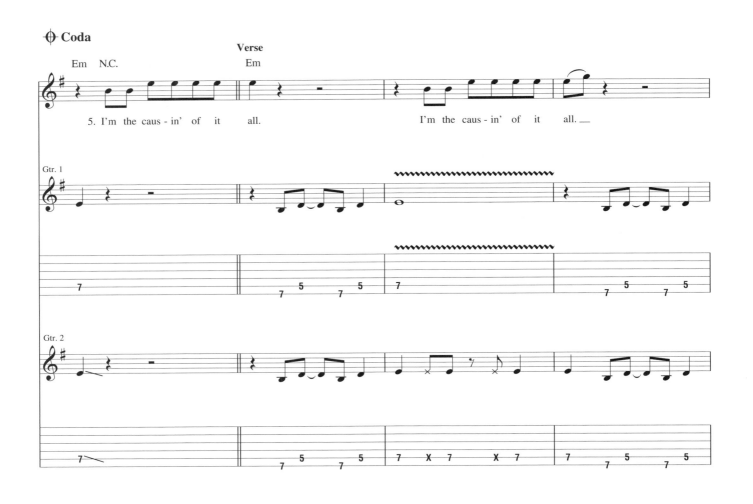

all. ____

I'm the caus-in' of it all. ____

I'm the caus-in' of it all. ____

Bm   Em   N.C.

Gtr. 3 (dist.)

Gtr. 1

Rhy. Fill 1   End Rhy. Fill 1

Gtr. 2

Outro-Guitar Solo

Gtr. 1: w/ Rhy. Fig. 1
Gtr. 2: w/ Rhy. Fig. 3

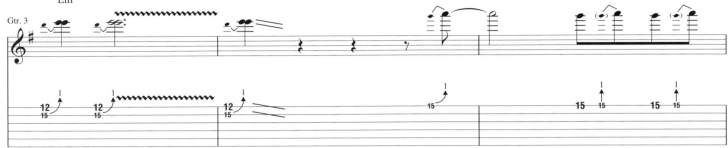

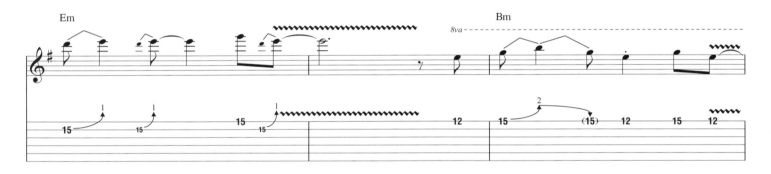

Gtr. 1: w/ Rhy. Fill 1
Gtr. 3: w/ Rhy. Fig. 3 (last meas.)

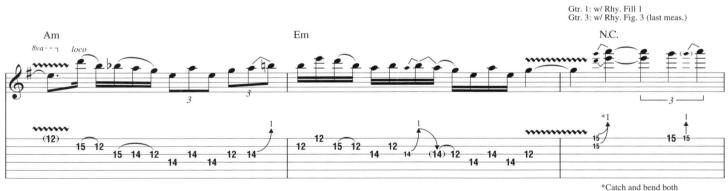

Gtr. 1: w/ Rhy. Fig. 1 (1st 9 meas.)
Gtr. 2: w/ Rhy. Fig. 3 (1st 9 meas.)

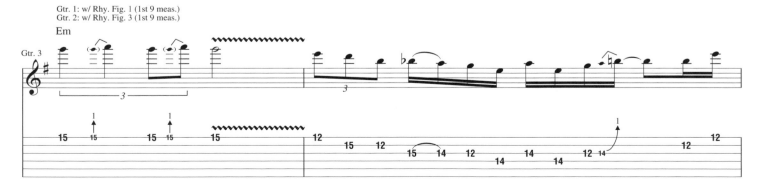

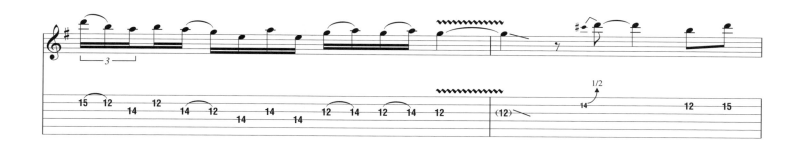

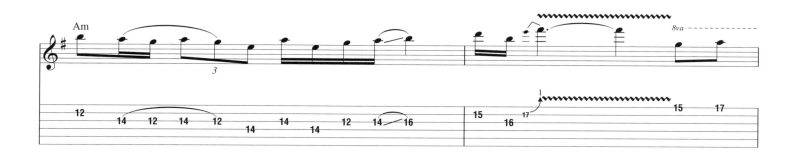

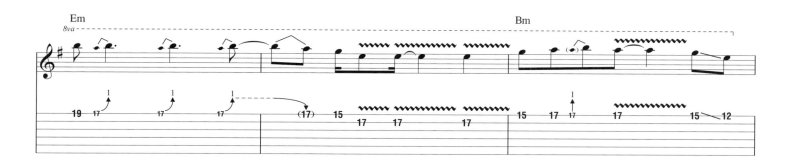

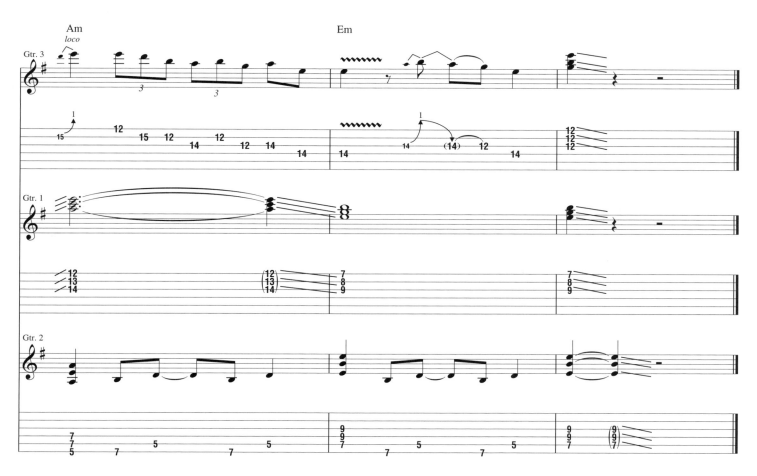

I GOT ALL YOU NEED

Written by Willie Dixon

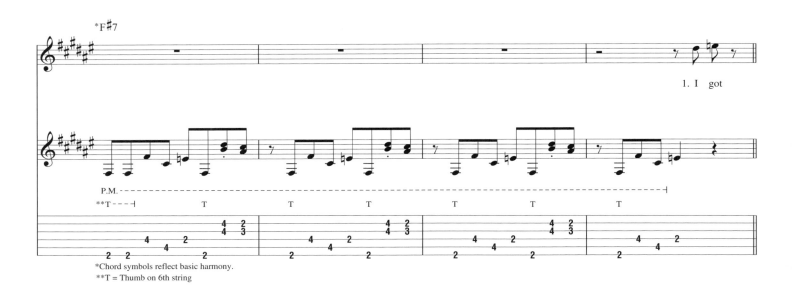

*Chord symbols reflect basic harmony.

**T = Thumb on 6th string

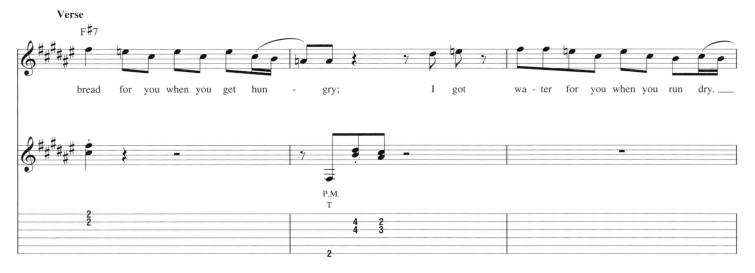

I got good times when you get lone - some; I got

heav - en be - fore you die. I got all you need.

I got all you need. And if you

wan - na have fun, ba - by, please make it to me.

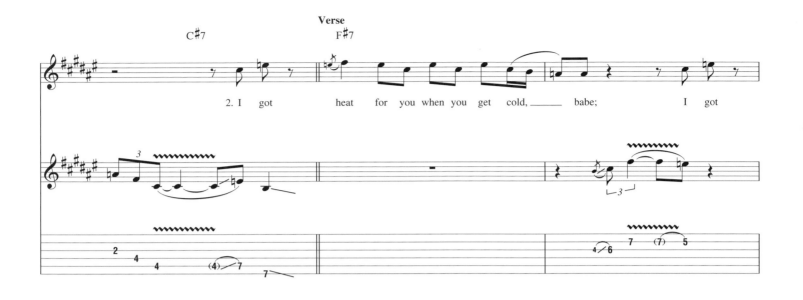

2. I got heat for you when you get cold, _____ babe; I got

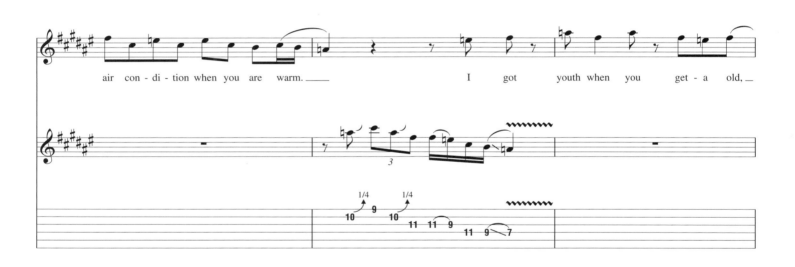

air con - di - tion when you are warm. ____ I got youth when you get - a old, _

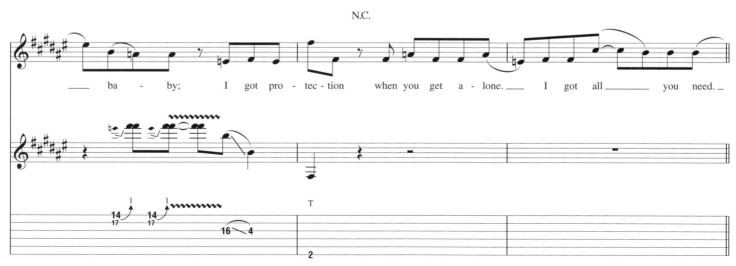

___ ba - by; I got pro - tec - tion when you get a - lone. _ I got all _____ you need. _

Chorus

I got all___ you need. ___ And if you

wan - na have fun, ___ ba - by, please make it to me. ___

Guitar Solo

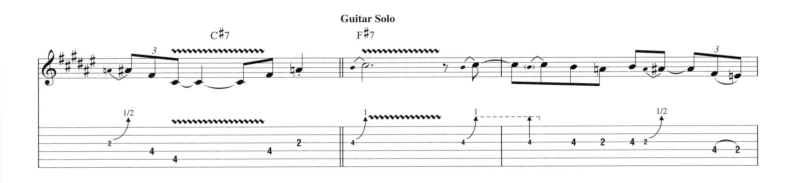

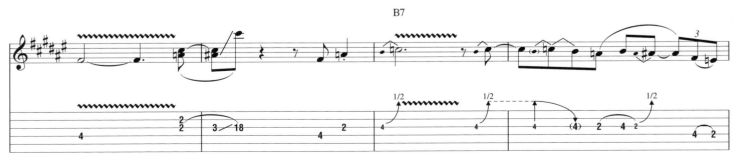

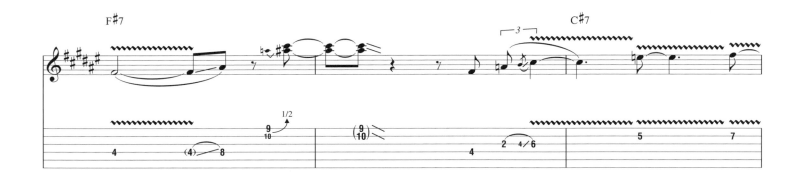

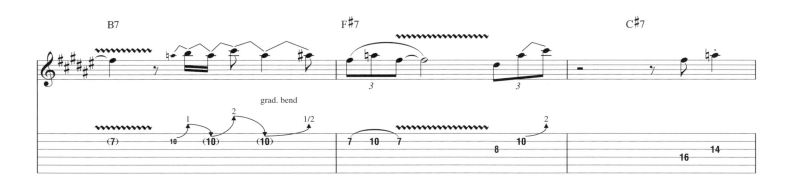

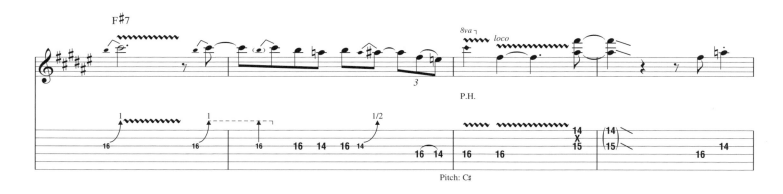

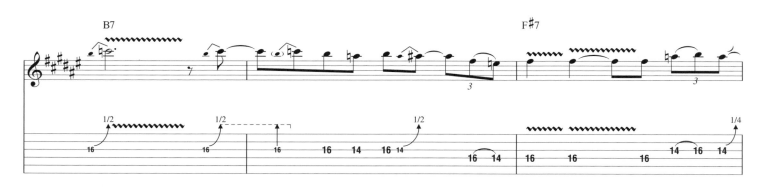

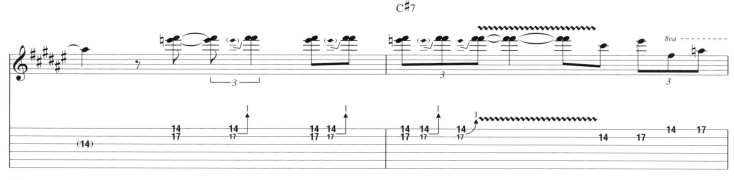

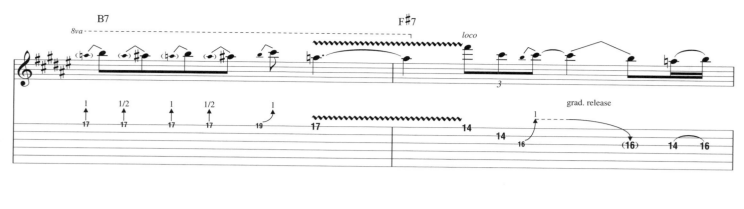

Verse

3. I got rhy-thm when you wan - na dance, ___ ba - by; I got a

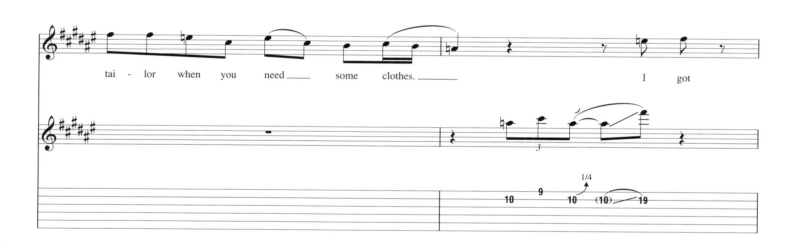

tai - lor when you need ___ some clothes. ___ I got

love for you when you get a lone - some; ___ I got mon - ey when you are broke. ___

I got all _____ you need. _____   I got all ___

_____ you need. _____   And if you wan-na have fun, ___

ba - by, please make it to me. _____

PLACE IN MY HEART

Written by Bernie Mardsen

Intro
Slowly, in 4 ♩ = 52

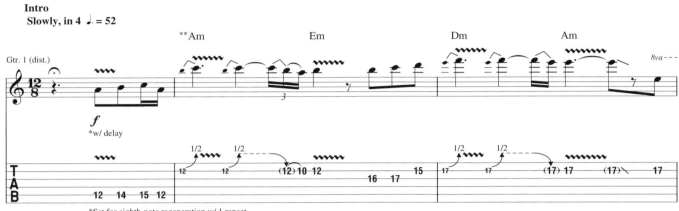

*Set for eighth-note regeneration w/ 1 repeat.
**Chord symbols reflect overall harmony.

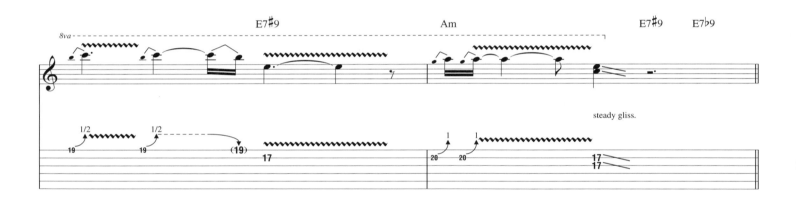

Verse
Gtr. 1 tacet
Am

1. Some - times I won - der, _____ what am I gon - na do? _____

***T = Thumb on 6th string

54

Verse

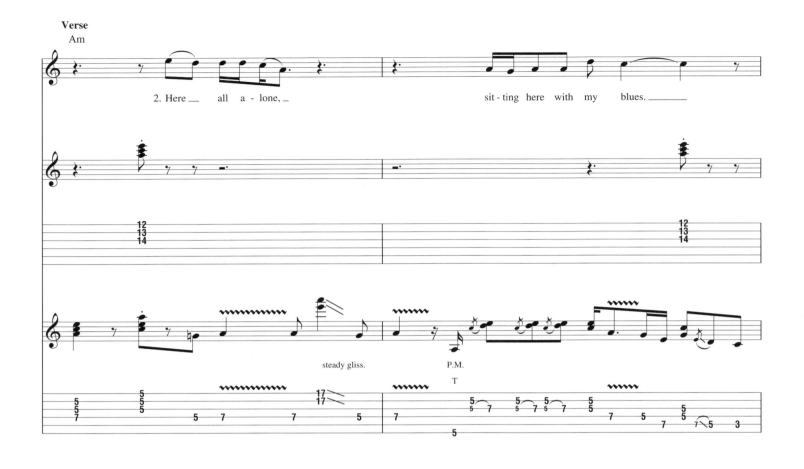

2. Here _ all a-lone, _ sit-ting here with my blues. _____

steady gliss.   P.M.

A-lone, ___ cold and scared _ now, babe. _ Oh, I've been miss-ing you. _____

let ring - - - - ⌐

56

Be-lieve me when I tell you now, dar-ling, _____ this hurt is for _ real. _____

Oh, it's time for me to start o - ver, _____ go and get some-thing new. _____

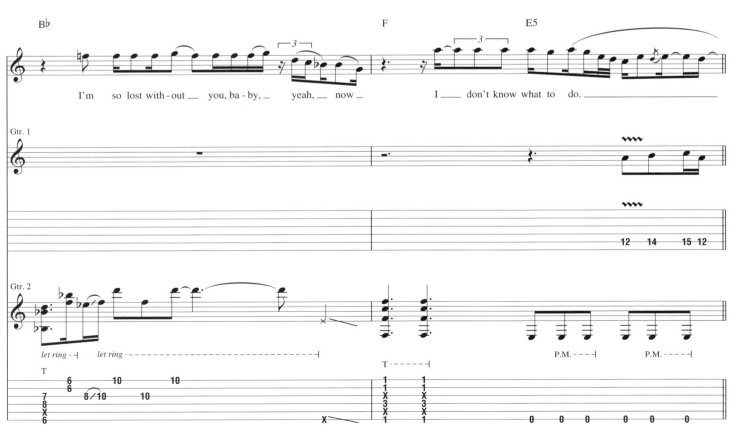

I'm so lost with-out _ you, ba-by, _ yeah, _ now _ I _ don't know what to do. _____

58

Interlude

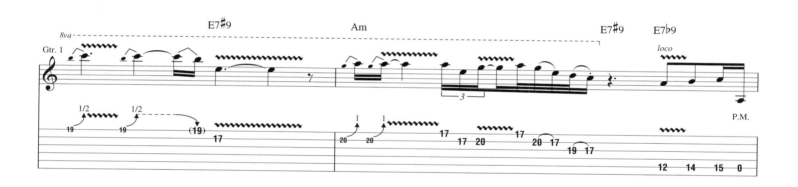

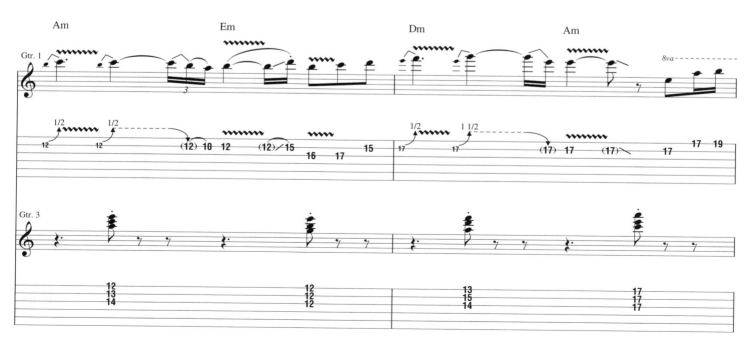

Guitar Solo

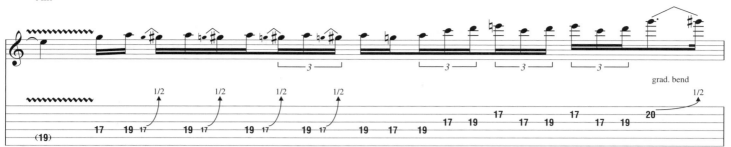

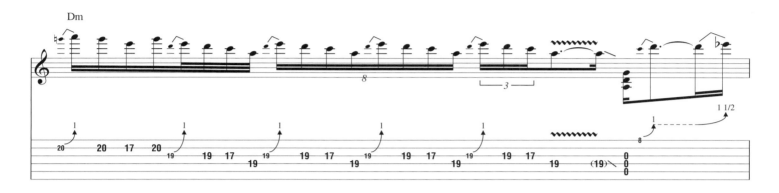

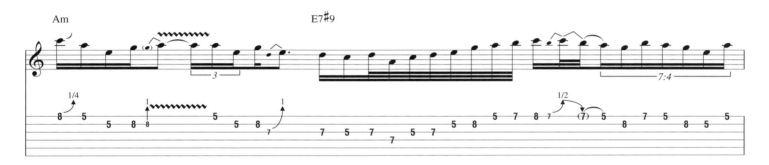

3. Some - times I won - der, _____ oh, ___ what I'm gon - na do. _____

Some-times I'm a-fraid, _ dar - ling. _   Oh, I'm still look-ing for _ you. _____

No mat-ter who you _ are, _____   ain't no mat-ter what you _ do, _____   there's a

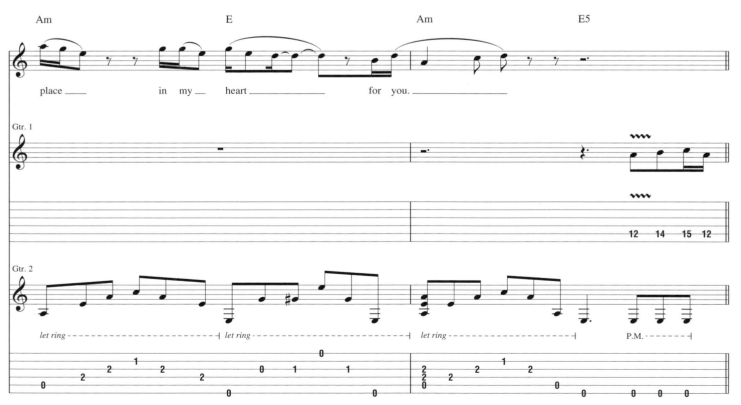

place _____   in my _ heart _____   for you. _____

I've __ seen __ trou-ble come.

All the tears I've cried. ____

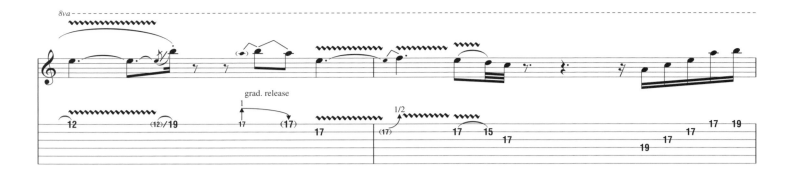

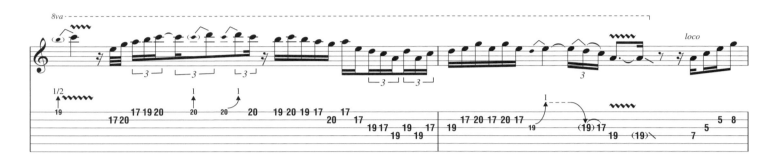

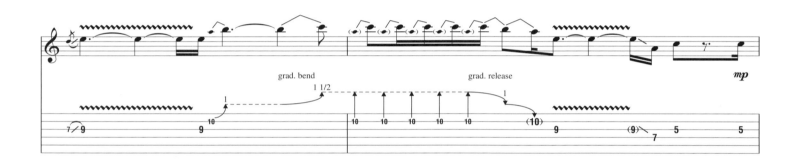

grad. bend

grad. release

*Pluck w/ middle finger.

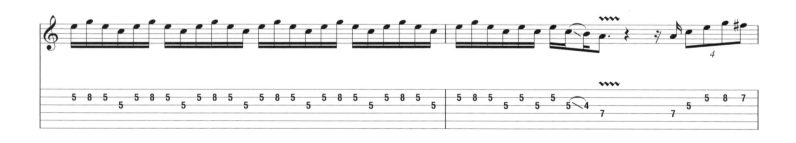

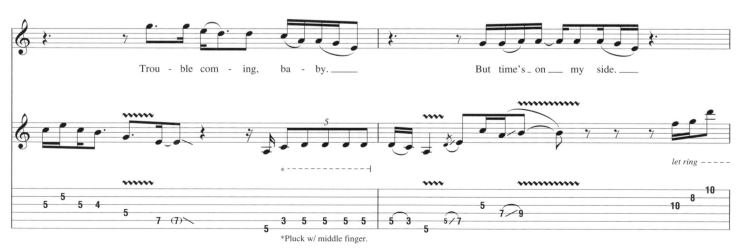

Trou - ble com - ing, ba - by. _____ But time's _ on __ my __ side. _____

let ring - - - -

There's a place in my heart _____

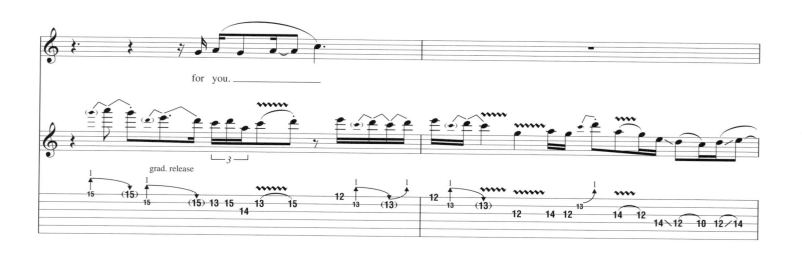

for you. _____

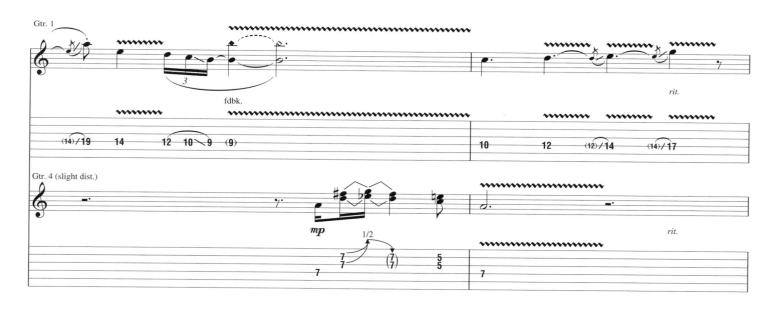

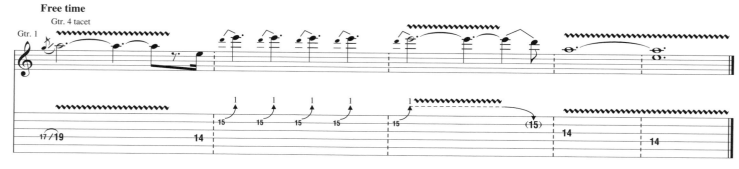

65

LONELY TOWN LONELY STREET

Words and Music by
Bill Withers

Verse

1st time, Gtr. 3 tacet

1st time, Gtr. 3: w/ Rhy. Fig. 2
3rd time, Gtr. 3: w/ Rhy. Fill 2

1st & 3rd times, Gtr. 3: w/ Rhy. Fig. 1

_____ in the crowd - ed ____ streets.
____ you _ can't   keep _ your   seat. ____
____ stone ex - pert at   kiss - ing.

F#5

But ___ the cit - y   real - ly   ain't   no   big-
But ___ if danc - es don't ___ lead   to   ro - manc -
But ___ it don't _ do   too _ much good _ to be

Rhy. Fill 2

Gtr. 3

68

2nd time, Gtr. 3: w/ Rhy. Fig. 3
3rd time, Gtr. 3: w/ Rhy. Fig. 3 (1st 3 meas.)

1st time, Gtr. 3: w/ 2nd measure of Rhy. Fig. 3
2nd time, Gtr. 1: w/ Rhy. Fill 1

- ger _____
- es,
talk - ing,   yeah, _____

than __ the   friend - ly   peo -
might __ as   well __ be   born, __
broth - er,   when __ there   ain't __

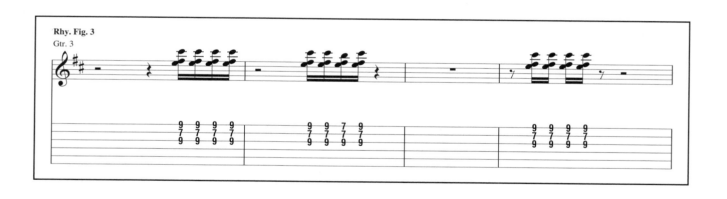

Rhy. Fig. 3
Gtr. 3

Rhy. Fill 1
Gtr. 1

70

Interlude

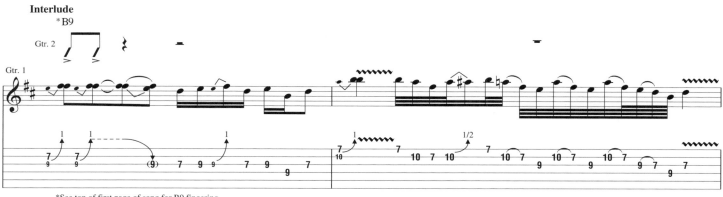

*See top of first page of song for B9 fingering.

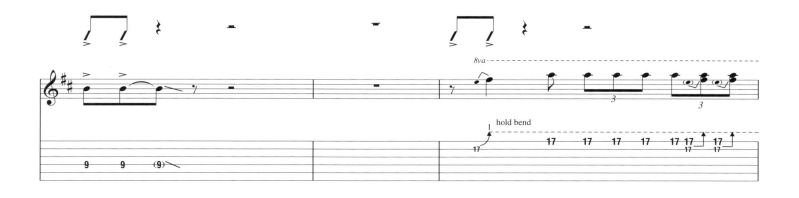

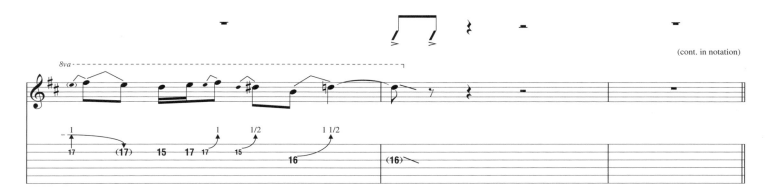

Guitar Solo

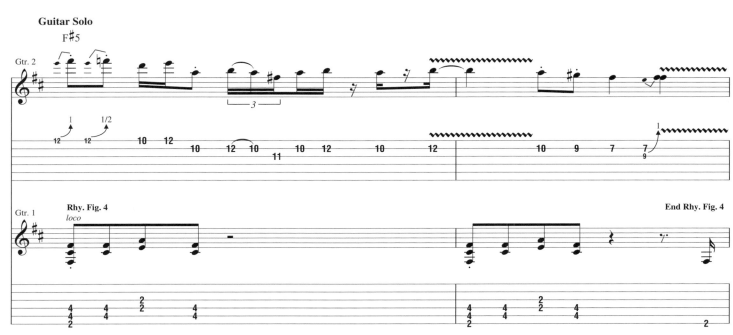

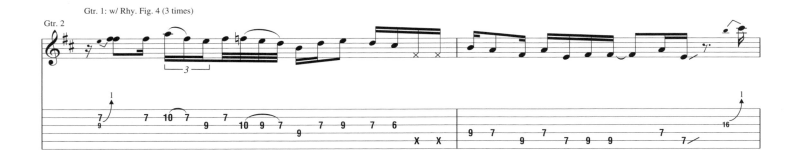

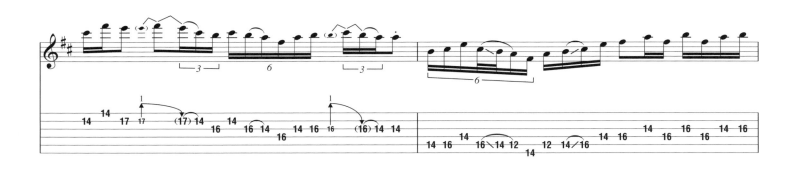

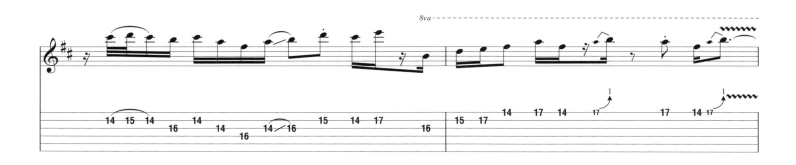

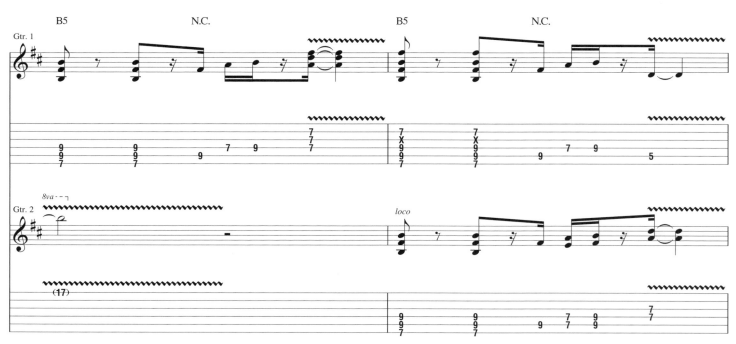

4. And _ if you _ are shy, _____ just not much of a talk - er, _____

don't _ im - press _ the peo - ple _____ that you meet,

F#5

you might as   well ____ be _

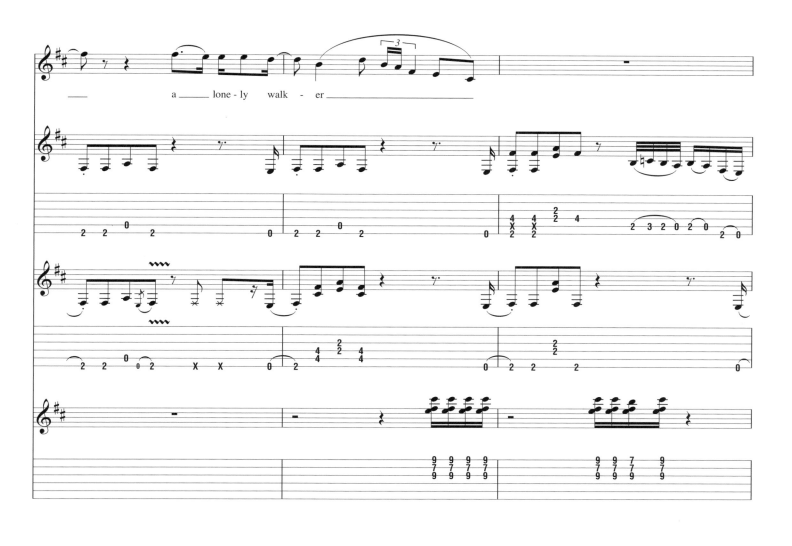

a ____ lone - ly walk - er _____

B5   N.C.

in ____ a lone - ly town ____   on a lone - ly street, ____

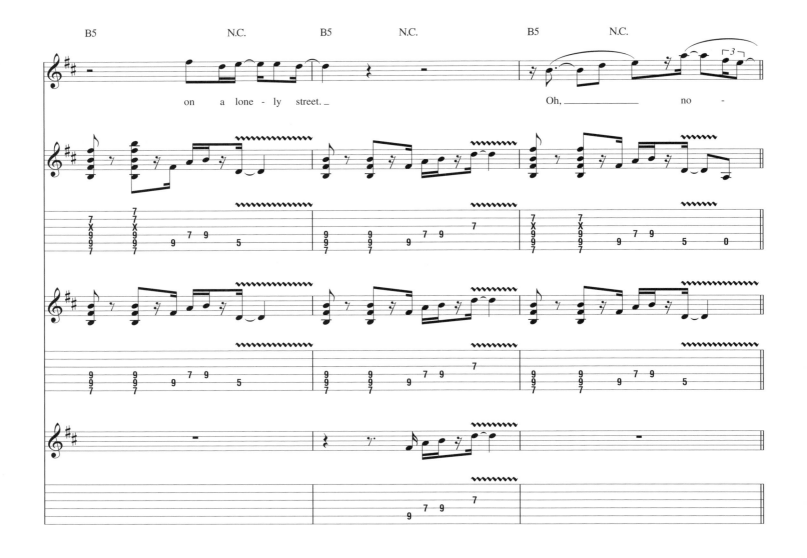

on a lone-ly street. _ Oh, _____ no -

Outro

Gtr. 3 tacet

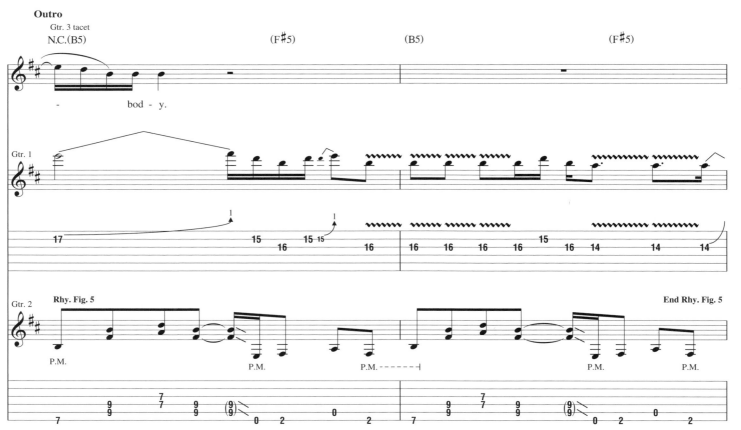

- bod - y.

Gtr. 1

Gtr. 2 Rhy. Fig. 5   End Rhy. Fig. 5

P.M.   P.M.   P.M. - - - - -| P.M.   P.M.

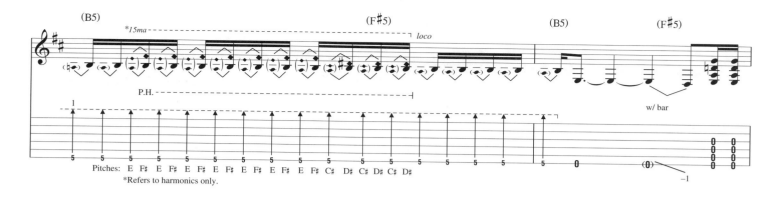

Pitches: E F♯ E F♯ E F♯ E F♯ E F♯ E F♯ E F♯ C♯ D♯ C♯ D♯ C♯ D♯
*Refers to harmonics only.

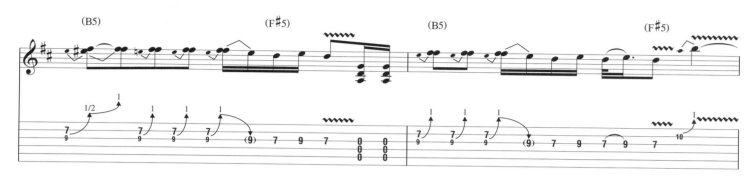

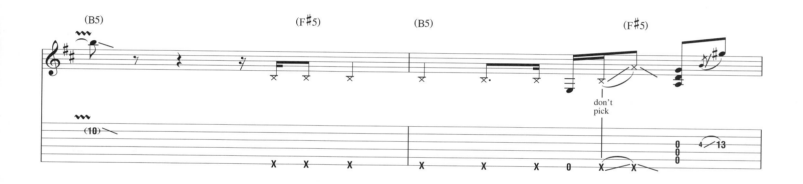

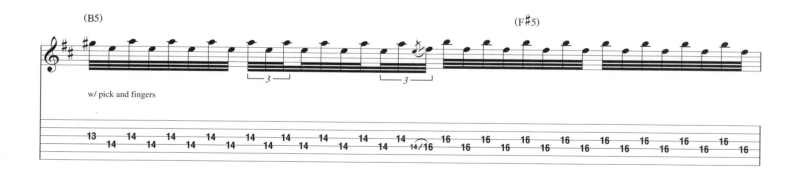

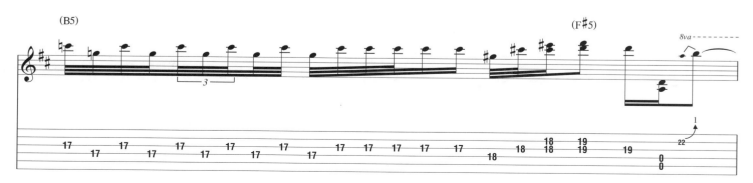

HEAVENLY SOUL

Words and Music by
Joe Bonamassa

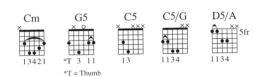

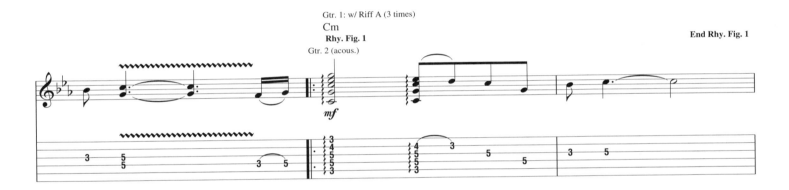

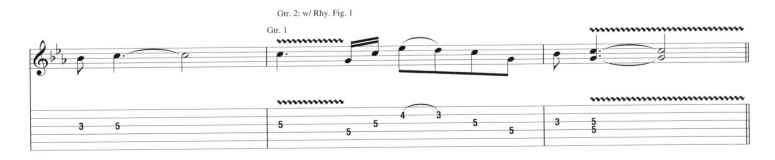

Chorus

*Cm

Rhy. Fig. 2A

Gtr. 2

Heav - en - ly soul, _____
(Heav - en - ly soul, _____

**Gtr. 3   Riff B

p

**Gtr. 4   Riff B1

p

Gtr. 1   Rhy. Fig. 2

*See top of first page of song for chord diagrams pertaining to rhythm slashes.
**Mandolin arr. for gtr.

heav - en - ly soul. _____
heav - en - ly soul.

End Riff B

End Riff B1

84

Interlude
Gtr. 2: w/ Rhy. Fig. 2A
*Gtrs. 3 & 4: w/ Riffs B & B1 (2 times)

*Played *mf* (till Guitar Solo).

Chorus
Gtr. 2: w/ Rhy. Fig. 2A
Gtrs. 3 & 4: w/ Riffs B & B1 (2 times)

But I know I'm bet - ter right now. ___ I was wrong. ___

Heav - en - ly soul,
(Heav - en - ly soul,

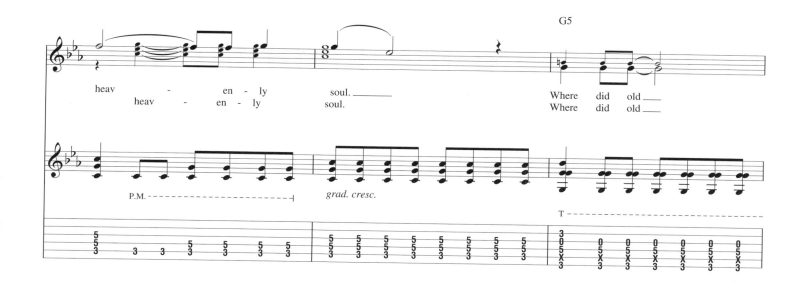

heav - en - ly soul. _____ Where did old ____
heav - en - ly soul. Where did old ____

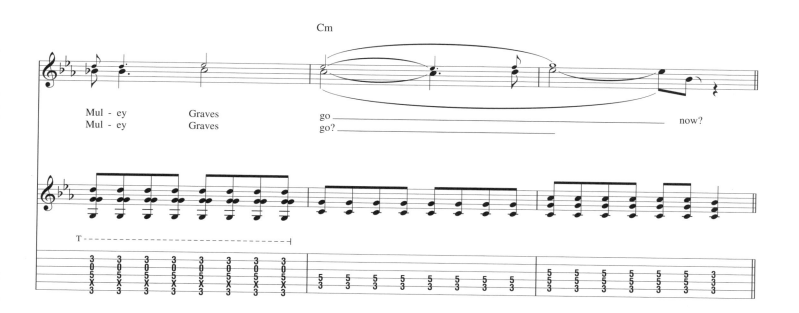

Mul - ey Graves go _____ now?
Mul - ey Graves go? _____

Guitar Solo

*When recalled first chord is played *mf*.

Gtr. 5

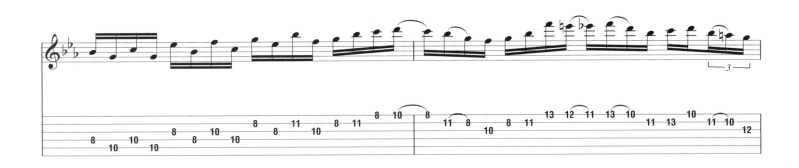

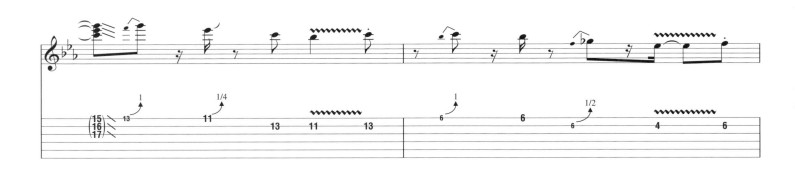

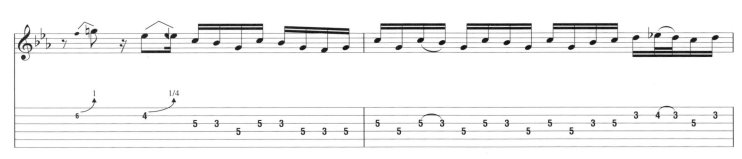

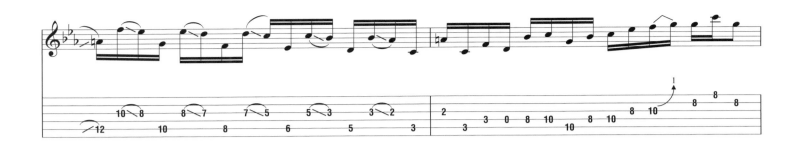

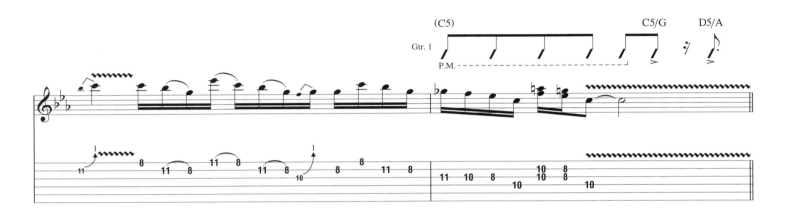

Interlude

Gtr. 1: w/ Rhy. Fig. 4
Gtr. 5 tacet

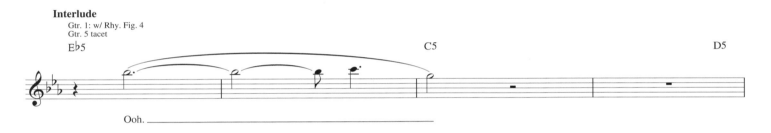

Eb5   C5   D5

Ooh.

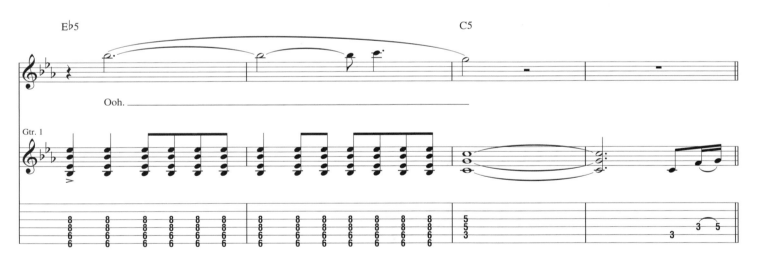

Eb5   C5

Ooh.

Gtr. 1

Outro

Gtr. 2: w/ Rhy. Fig. 1 (3 times)   *Gtr. 2: w/ Rhy. Fig. 1

Cm   Cm

Play 3 times

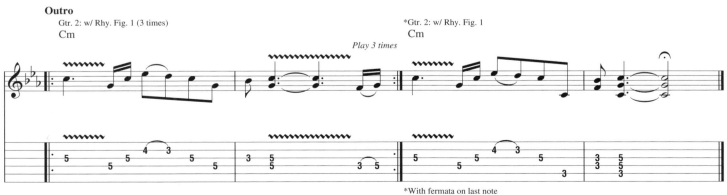

*With fermata on last note

NEW COAT OF PAINT

Words and Music by
Tom Waits

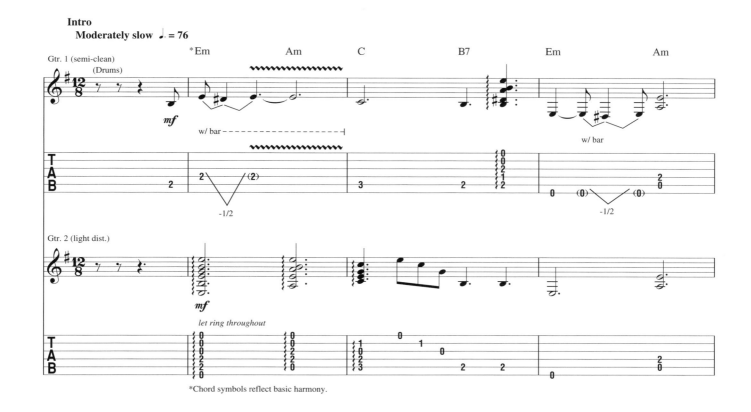

*Chord symbols reflect basic harmony.

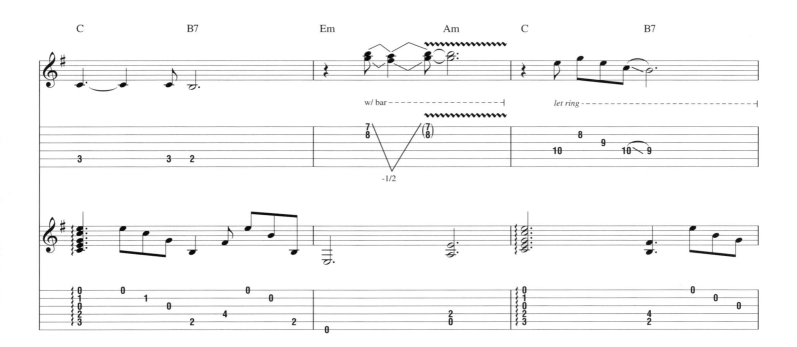

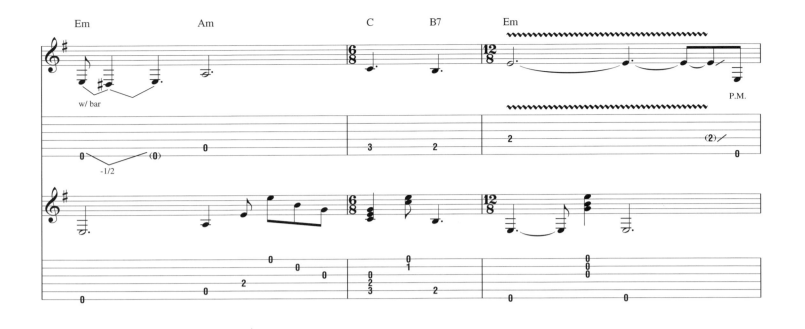

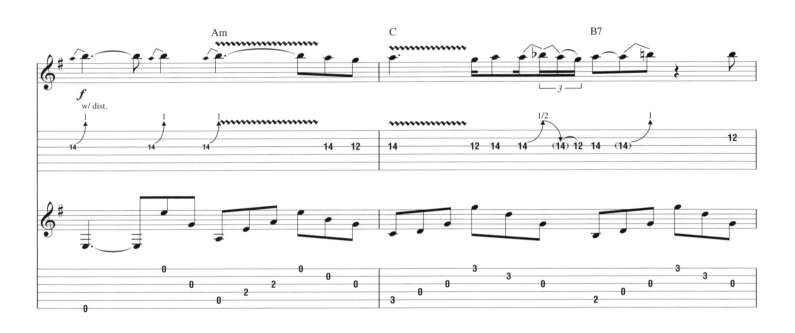

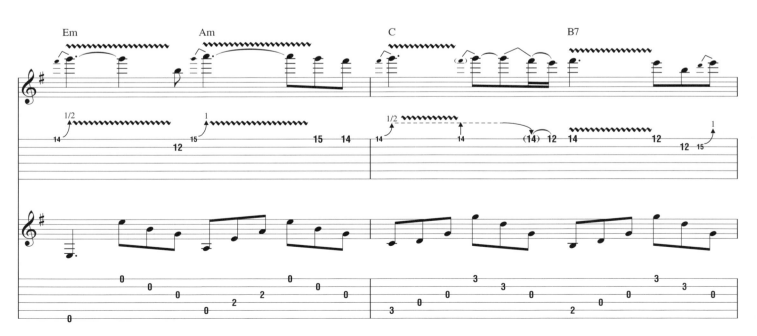

Verse

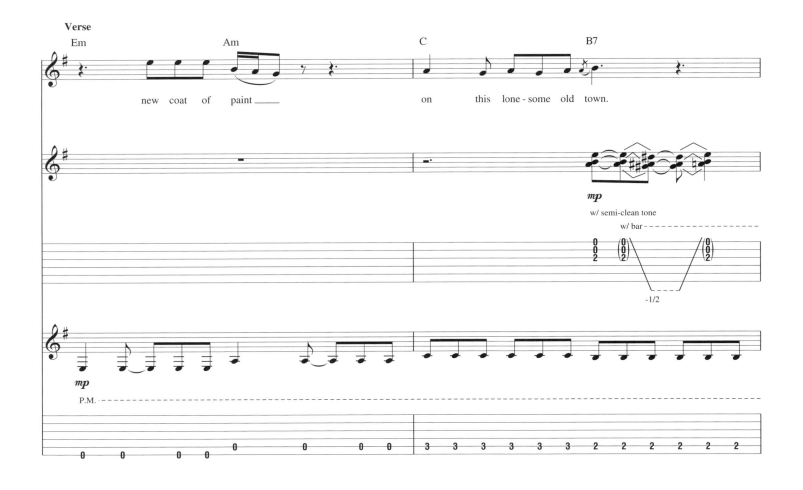

new coat of paint _____ on this lone - some old town.

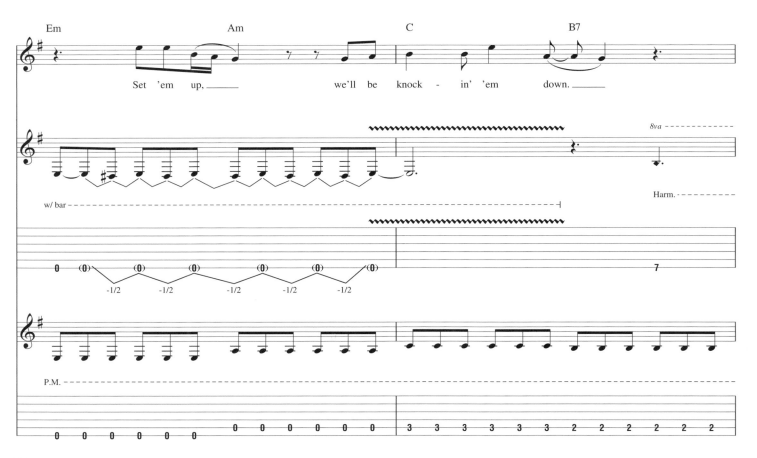

Set 'em up, _____ we'll be knock - in' 'em down. _____

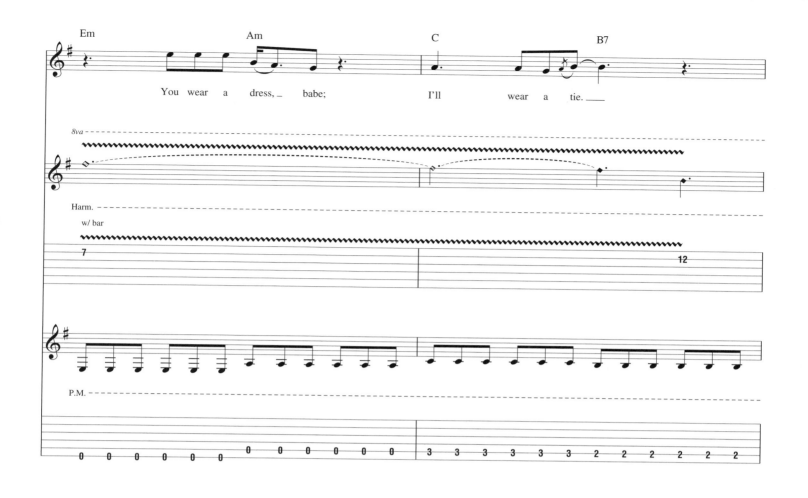

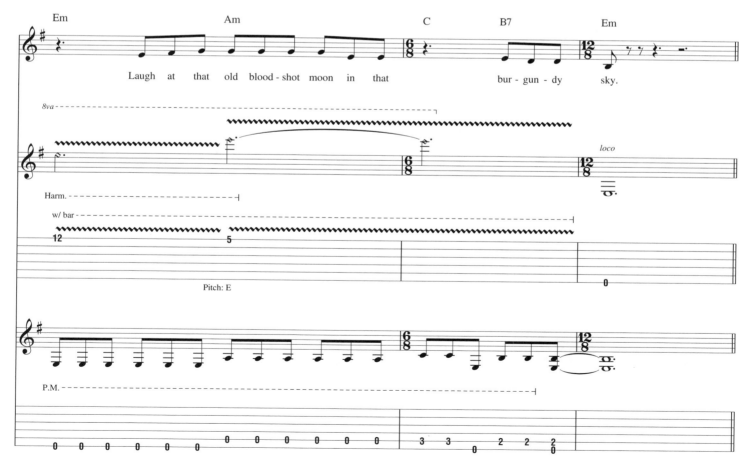

Interlude

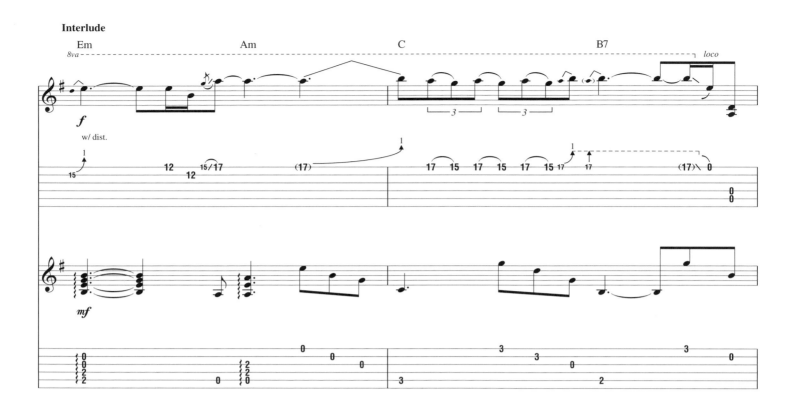

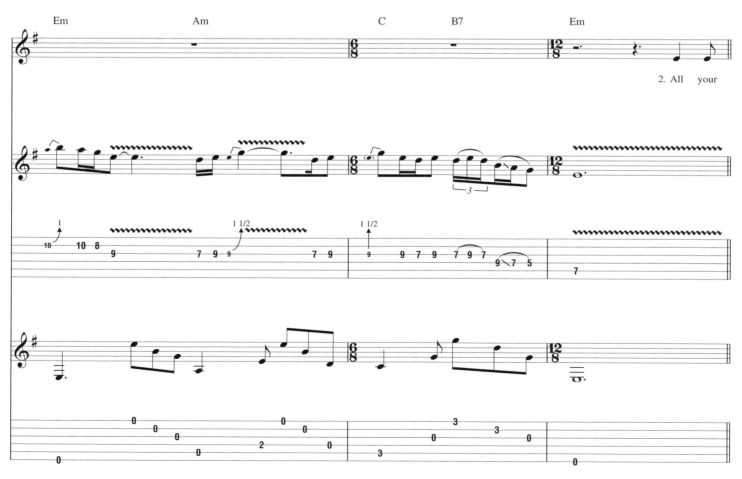

Verse

scrib - bled love ___ dreams are lost or thrown a - way, ___

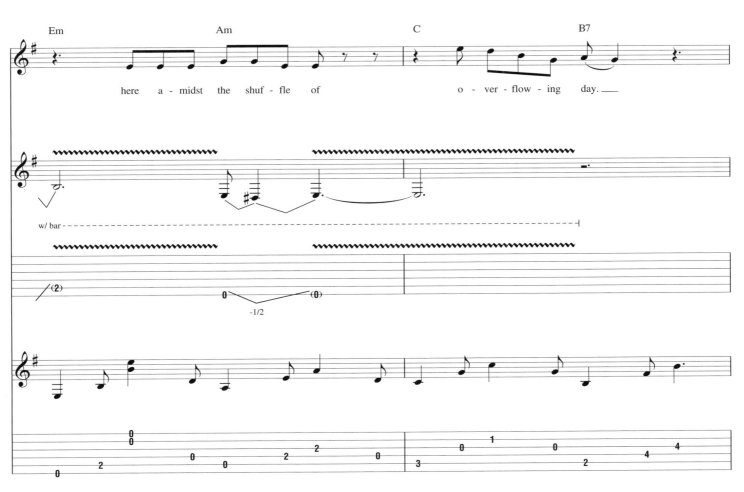

here a - midst the shuf - fle of o - ver - flow - ing day. ___

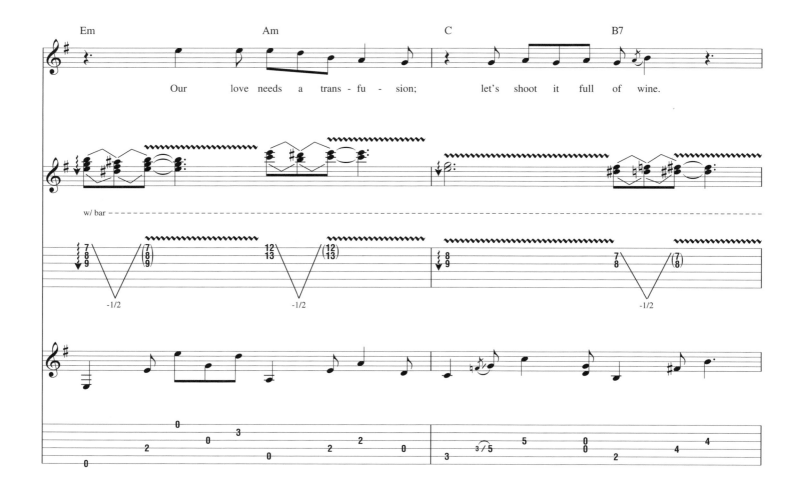

Our love needs a trans-fu-sion; let's shoot it full of wine.

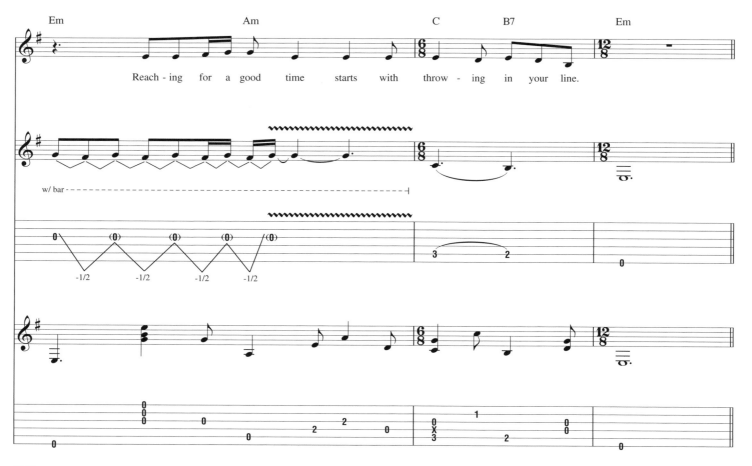

Reach-ing for a good time starts with throw-ing in your line.

Guitar Solo

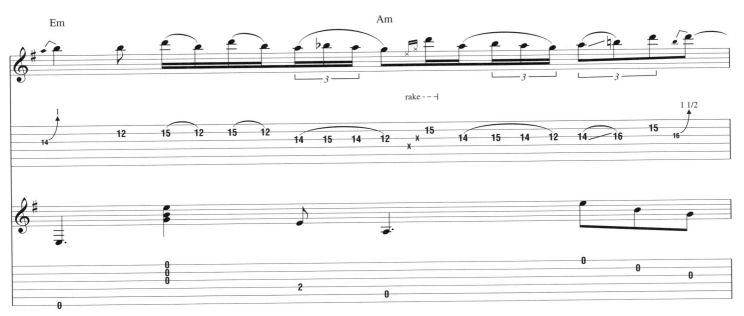

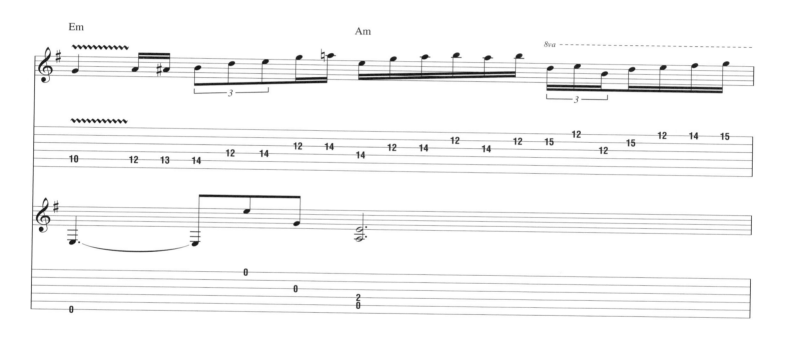

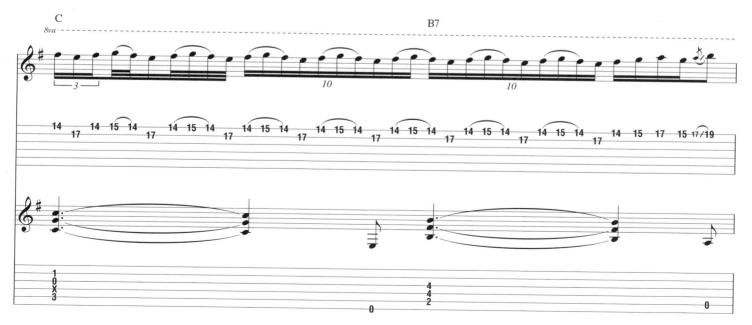

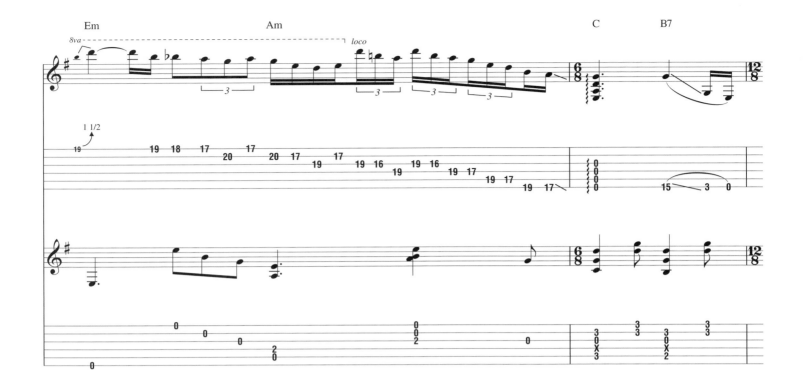

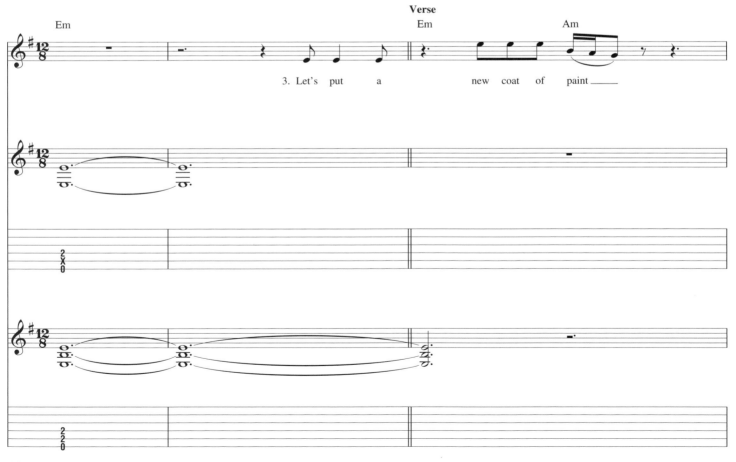

on this lone-some old ___ town.   Set 'em up, _____   we'll be

knock - in' 'em down. _____   You wear a dress, _ babe,

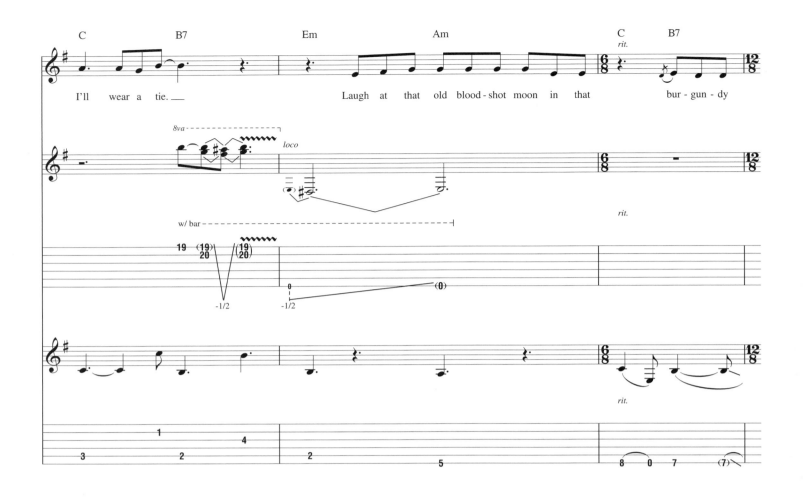

I'll wear a tie. ___   Laugh at that old blood-shot moon in that   bur-gun-dy

Free time

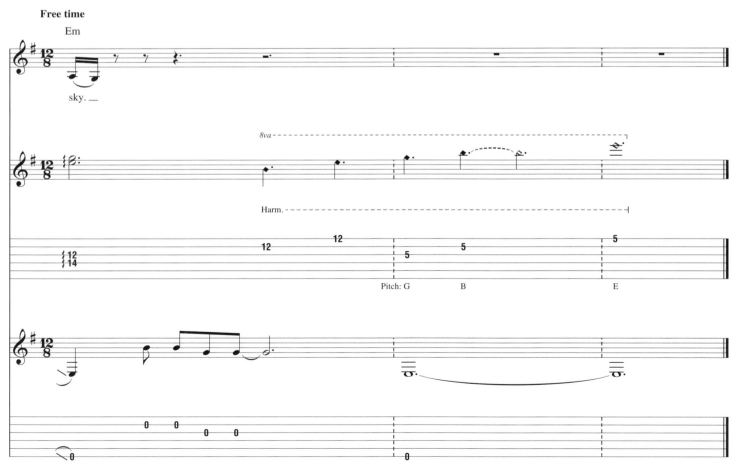

sky. ___

SOMEWHERE TROUBLE DON'T GO

Words and Music by
Joe Bonamassa

Open G tuning, capo V:
(low to high) D-G-D-G-B-D

Intro
Moderately ♩ = 120

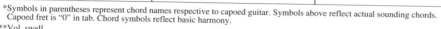

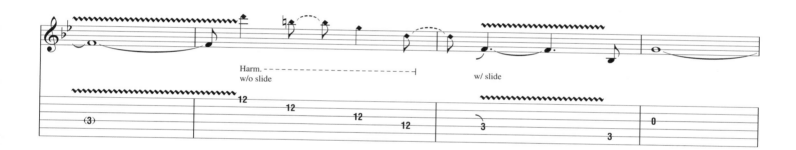

*Symbols in parentheses represent chord names respective to capoed guitar. Symbols above reflect actual sounding chords.
Capoed fret is "0" in tab. Chord symbols reflect basic harmony.
**Vol. swell

Dev - il had a daugh-ter, took me to the wa-ter, tried to kill ___ me with a kiss.

110

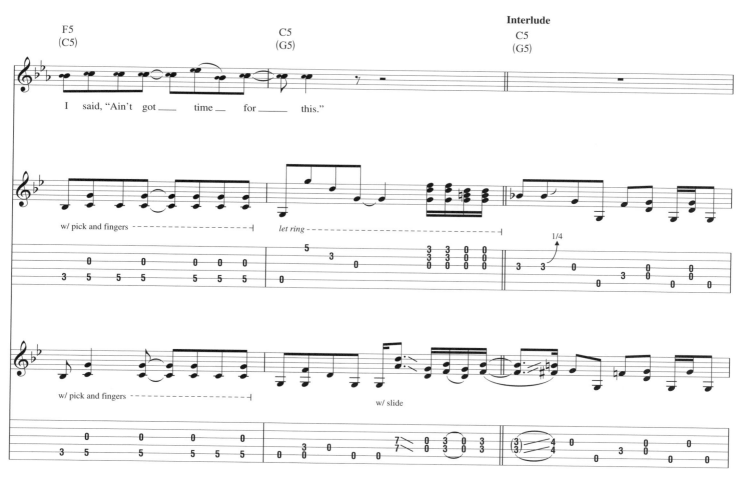

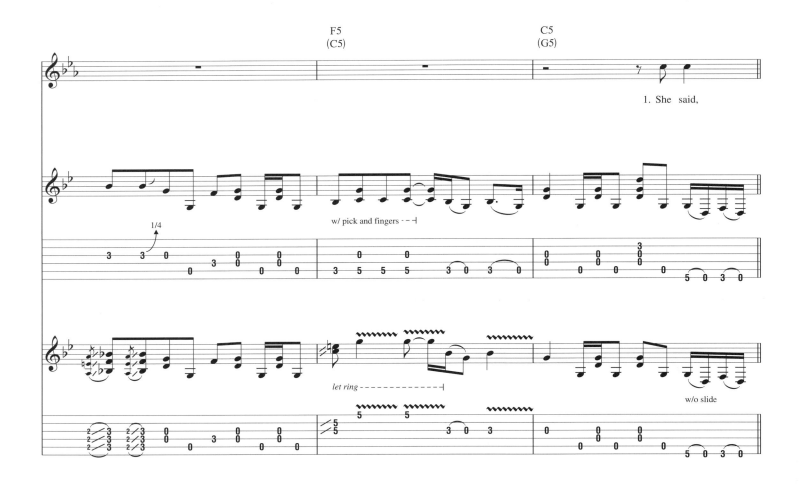

Verse

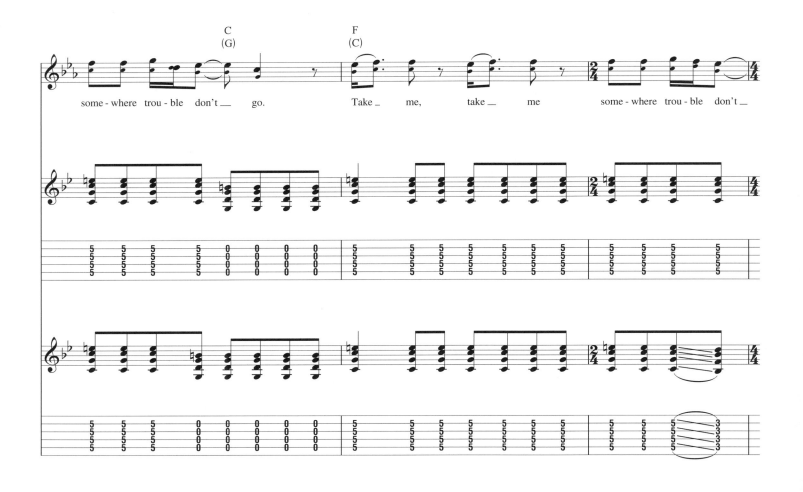

some - where trou - ble don't __ go.   Take __ me,   take __ me   some - where trou - ble don't __

Chorus

__ go. __   Dev - il had a daugh - ter,   took me to the wa - ter,

End Rhy. Fig. 1

P.M. -------------------
w/o slide

End Rhy. Fig. 1A

P.M. -------------------   P.M. -------------------
w/o slide

tried to kill ___ me with a kiss. _____ Said, "Hey now, hon - ey,

what a - bout the mon - ey?" I said, "Ain't got ___ time ___ for _____ this. No, got ___

Interlude

Verse

Chorus

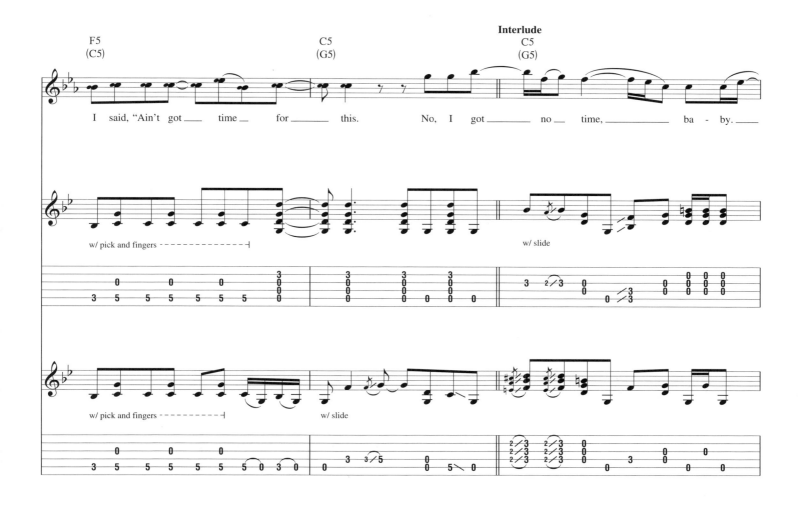

I said, "Ain't got ___ time ___ for ___ this. No, I got ___ no ___ time, ___ ba - by. ___

w/ pick and fingers ------------

w/ slide

w/ pick and fingers ------------

w/ slide

___ Not for you an - y - more." ___

let ring ------------------

Bridge

Take me, **take** me some-where trou-ble don't go. **Take** me, **take** me

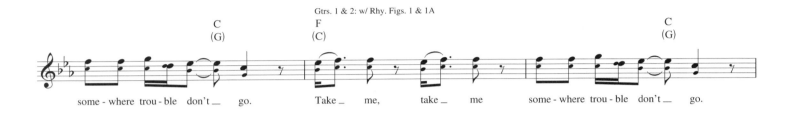

some-where trou-ble don't go. Take me, take me some-where trou-ble don't go.

Take me, take me some-where trou-ble don't go.

Chorus

Dev - il had a daugh-ter, took me to the wa-ter, tried to kill me with a kiss.

C5
(G5)

Take me back ___ home, ___ now.
Said, "Hey now, hon - ey, what a - bout the mon - ey?"

P.M. ----------------------------------

F5   C5
(C5)   (G5)

I said, "Ain't got ___ time ___ for ___ this."
Lord, I've ___ got ___ no ___ time, ___ ba - by.
Dev - il had a daugh - ter,

w/ pick and fingers ---------------

P.M. ----------------------

w/ pick and fingers ---

123

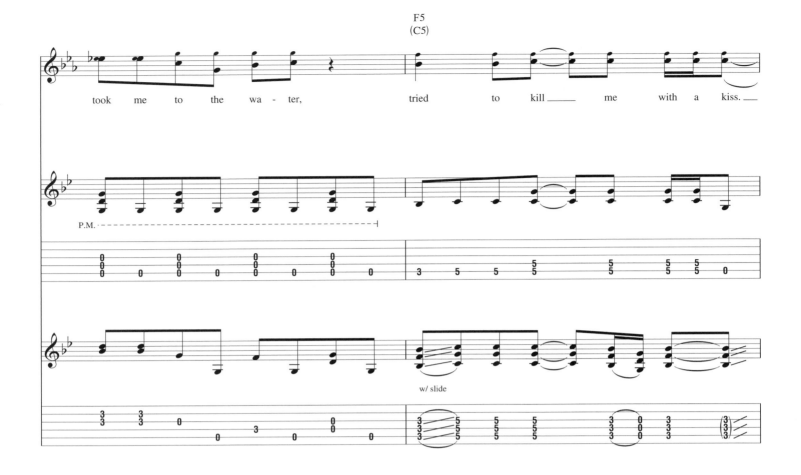

took me to the wa - ter,   tried   to   kill _____ me   with   a   kiss. ____

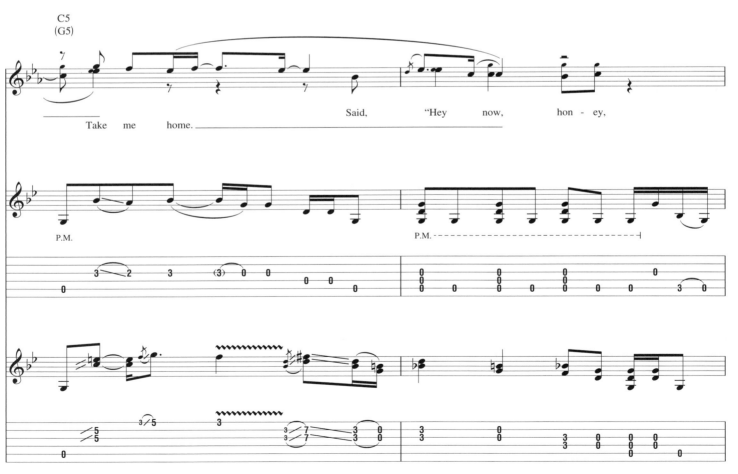

_____ Take   me   home. _____   Said,   "Hey   now,   hon - ey,

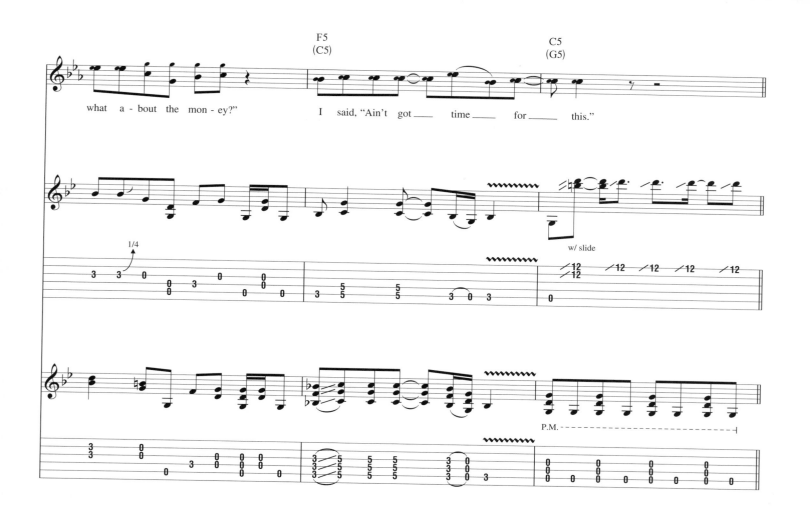

what a - bout the mon - ey?"   I said, "Ain't got _____ time _____ for _____ this."

Outro

Gtr. 2 tacet

C5
(G5)

Gtr. 1

F5
(C5)

C5
(G5)

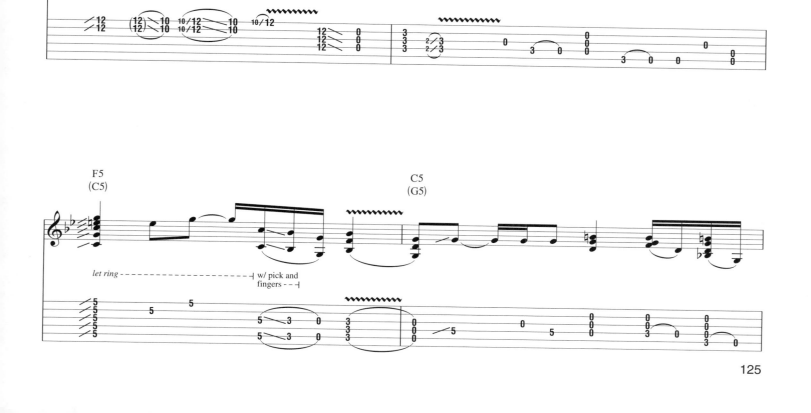

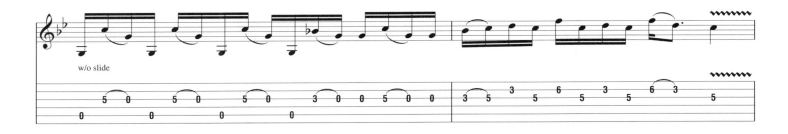

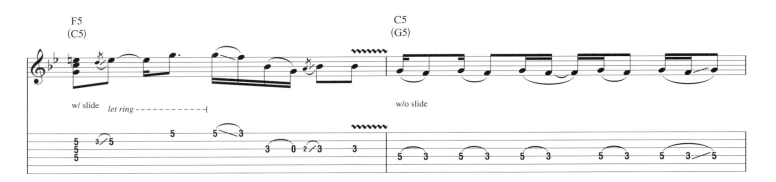

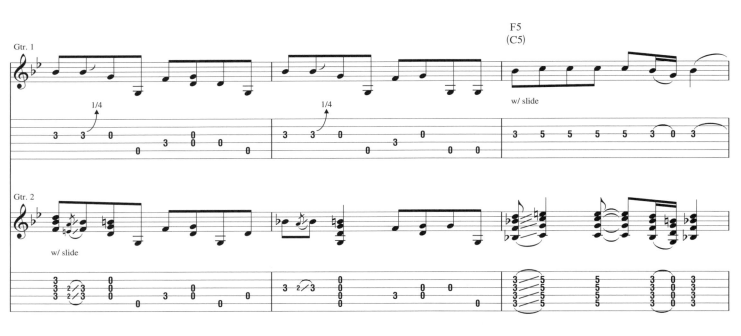

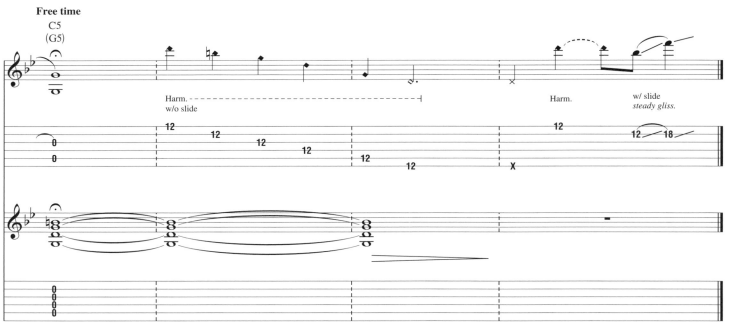

TOO MUCH AIN'T ENOUGH LOVE

Words and Music by Jonathan Cain,
Neal Schon, Jimmy Barnes,
Tony Brock and Randy Jackson

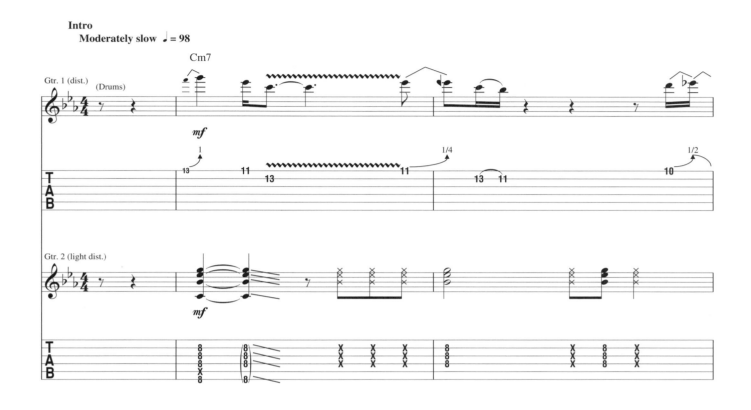

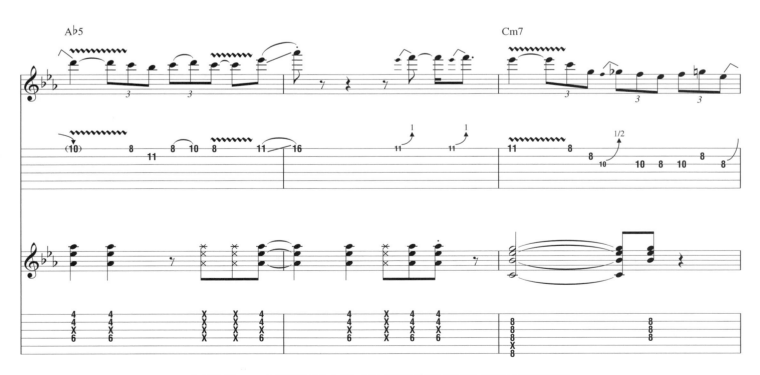

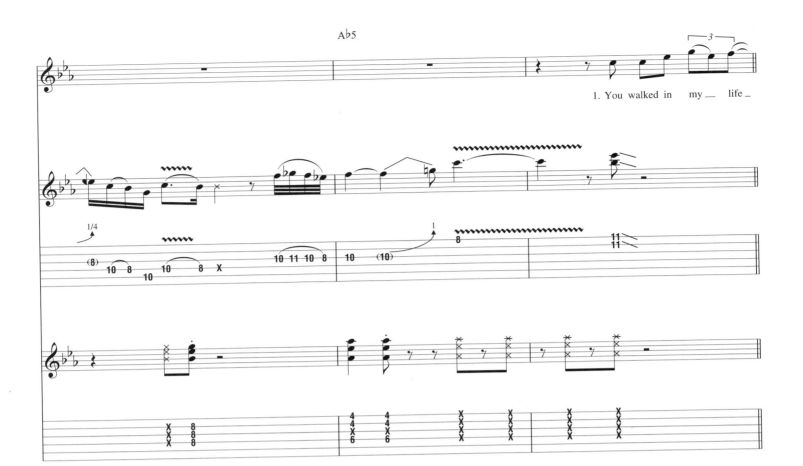

1. You walked in my — life —

Verse

with an an - gel's smile. _____

How could I have known _____ the hun - ger locked in - side? ___

We can start a fire, _____ but we

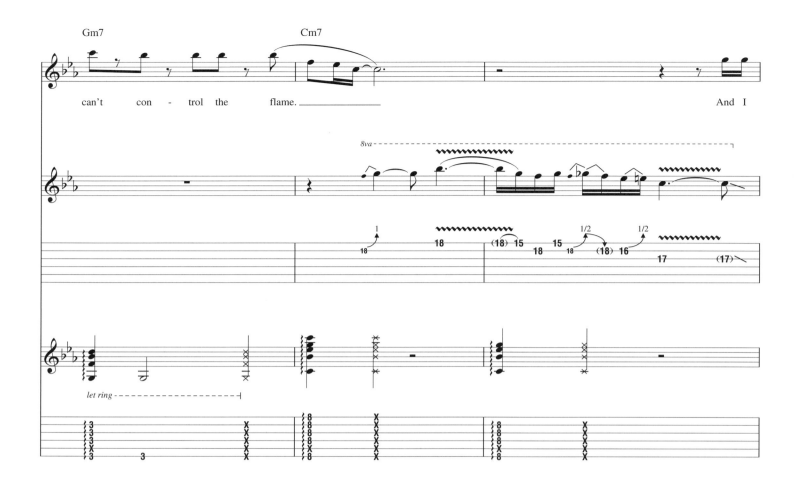

can't con - trol the flame.

And I

just can't __ wait __ to feel the heat a - gain. _____

In the

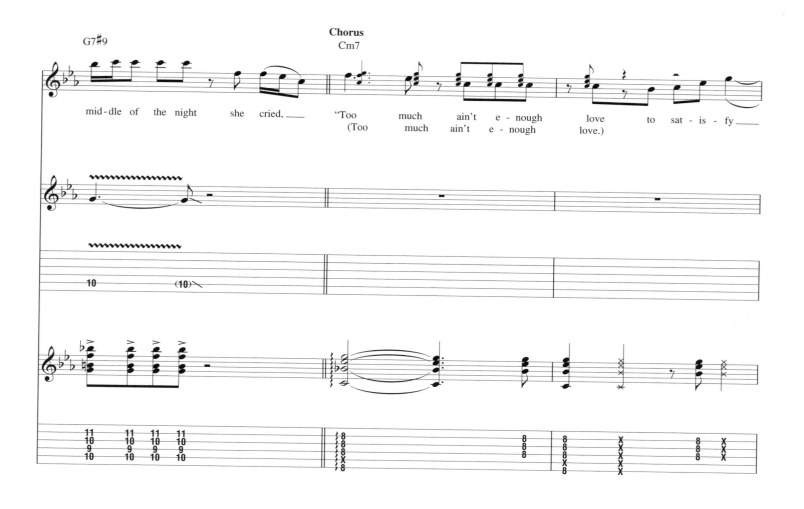

mid-dle of the night she cried, ___ "Too much ain't e-nough love to sat-is-fy ___
(Too much ain't e-nough love.)

___ me." ___ Yeah, ___ I said, "Too much ain't e-nough ___
(Too much ain't e-nough

Verse

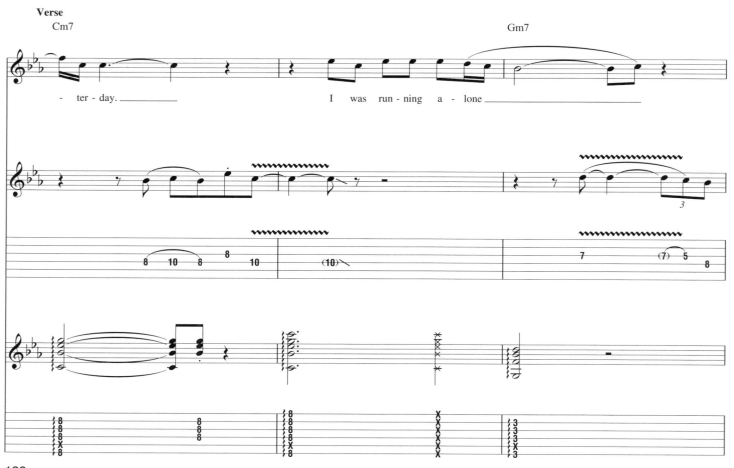

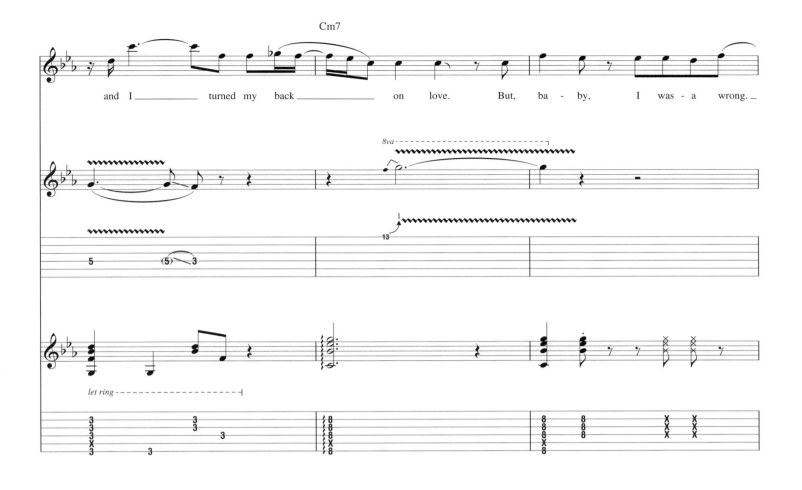

Cm7

and I _____ turned my back _____ on love. But, ba - by, I was - a wrong. ___

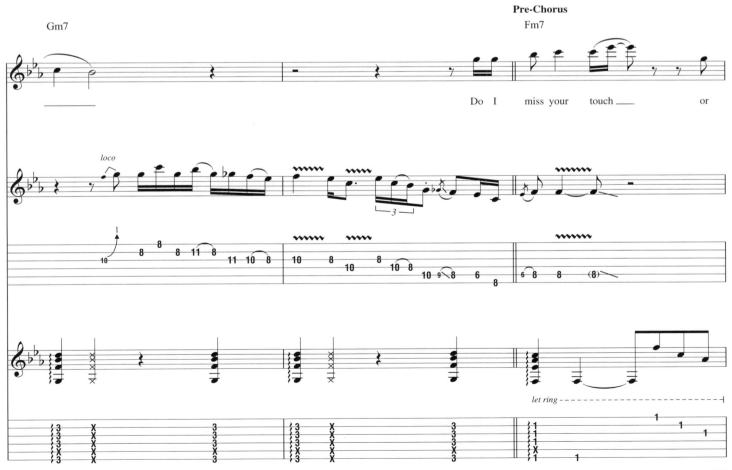

Gm7

Pre-Chorus

Fm7

___ and I ___

Do I miss your touch ___ or

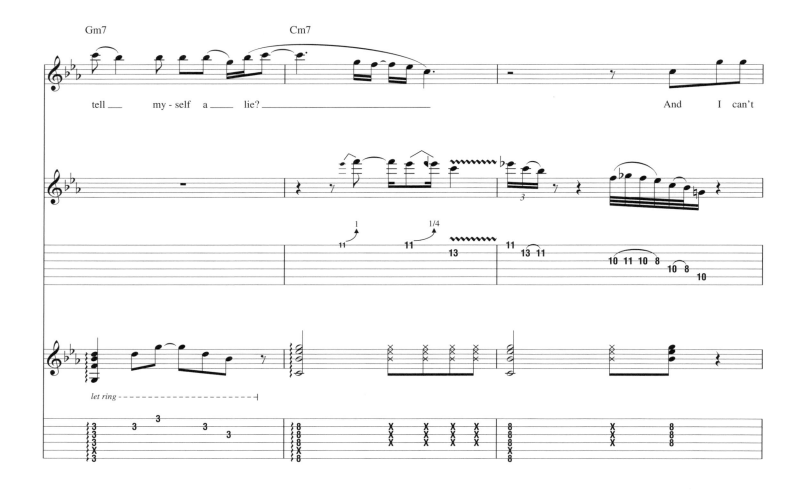

tell ___ my-self a ___ lie? _____ And   I   can't

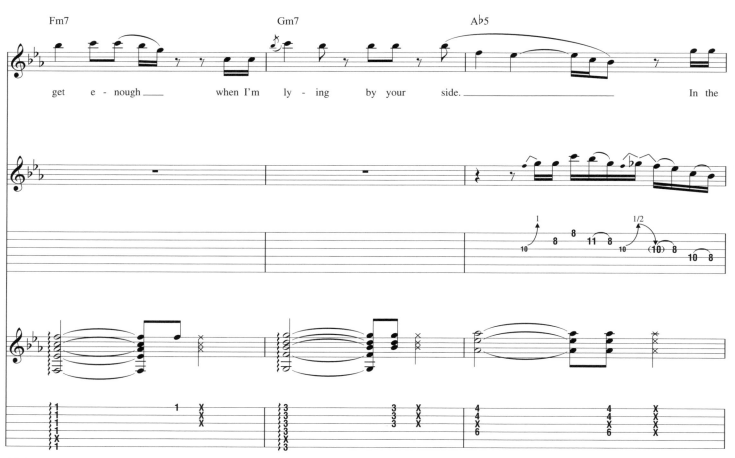

get   e - nough ___   when I'm   ly - ing   by your   side. _____ In the

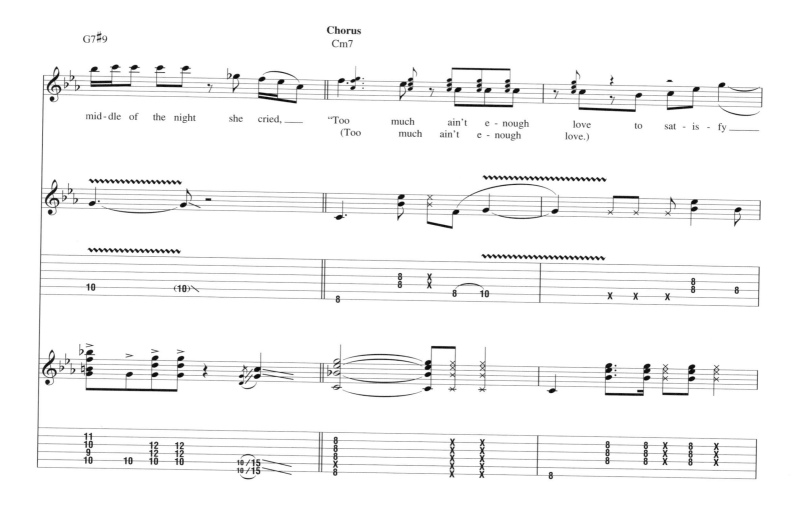

mid-dle of the night she cried, ___ "Too much ain't e-nough love to sat-is-fy ___
(Too much ain't e-nough love.)

me, yeah. Too much ain't e-nough
(Too much ain't e-nough

Ab5

love to sat - is - fy _____ me. _____ I got a burn - ing heart, _____ ba - by. _____
love.)

Guitar Solo

Cm7

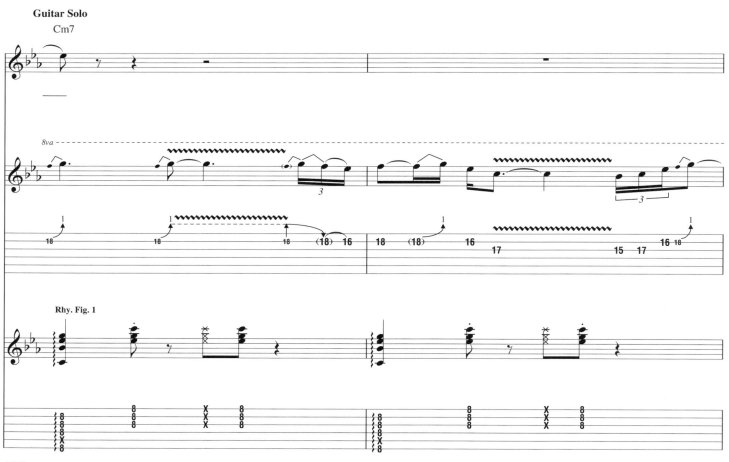

Rhy. Fig. 1

Gm7

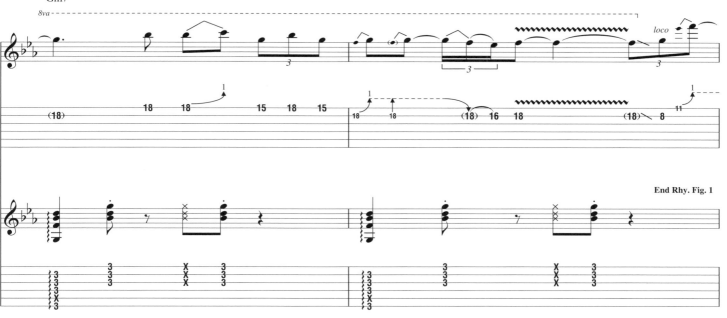

End Rhy. Fig. 1

Gtr. 2: w/ Rhy. Fig. 1

Cm7

Hoo,   hoo,   hoo.

Gtr. 1

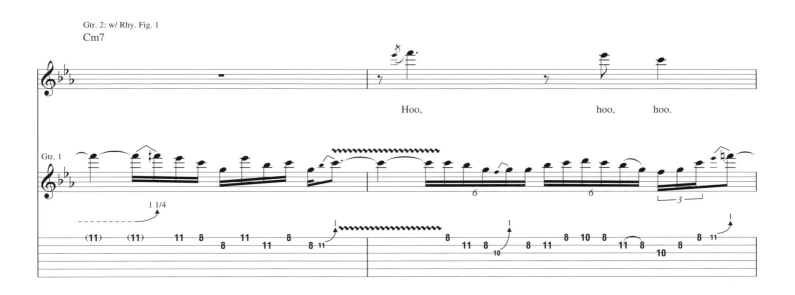

Gm7

Do I

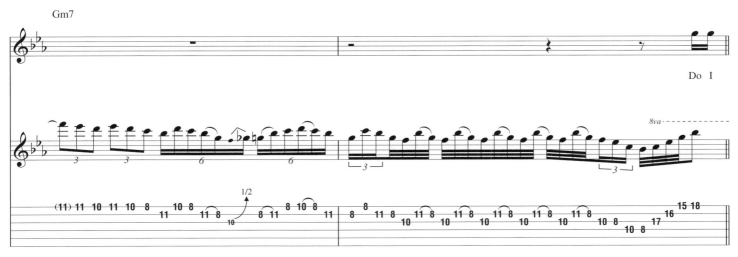

Pre-Chorus

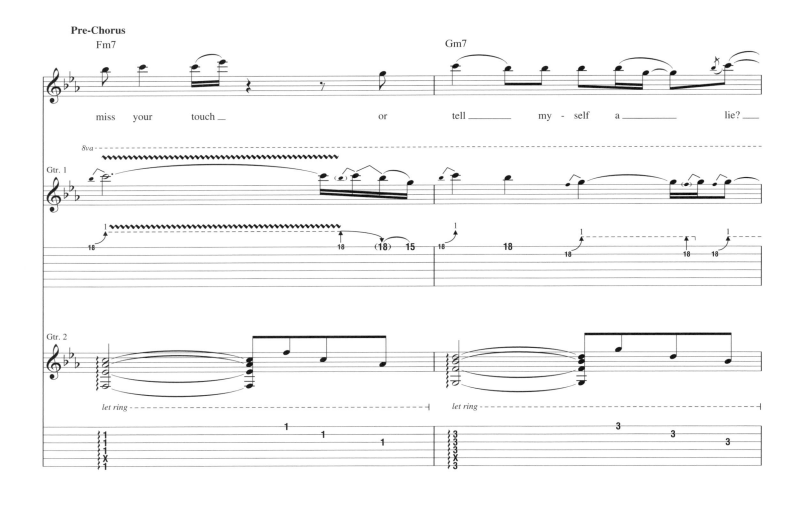

miss your touch ___ or tell ____ my - self a _____ lie? ___

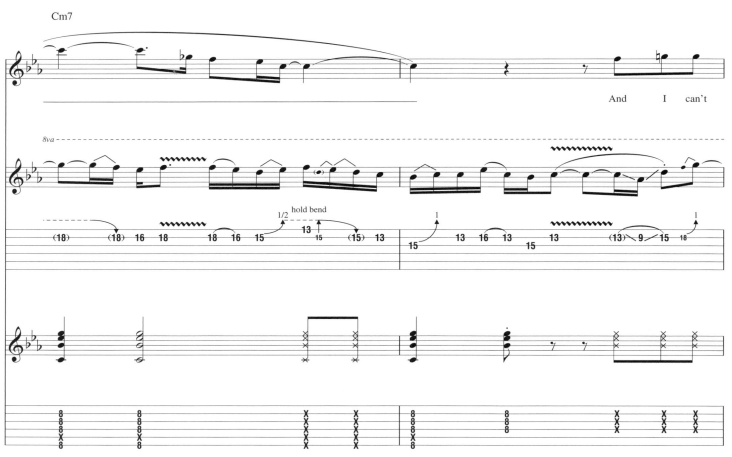

And I can't

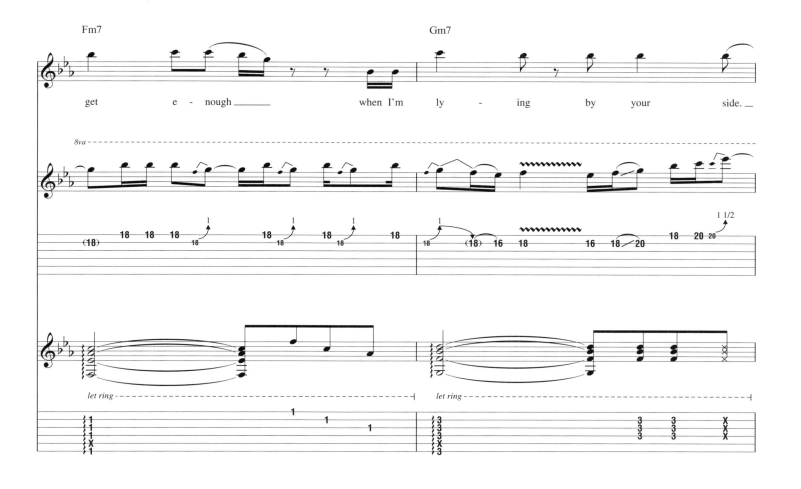

get e - nough _____ when I'm ly - ing by your side. _

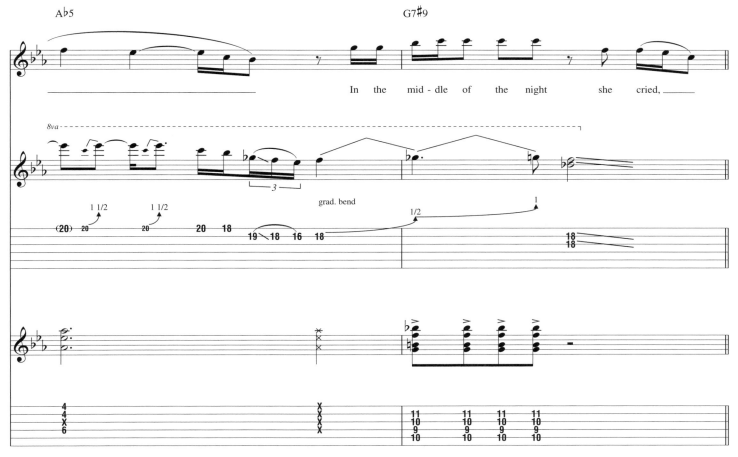

In the mid - dle of the night she cried, _____

Chorus

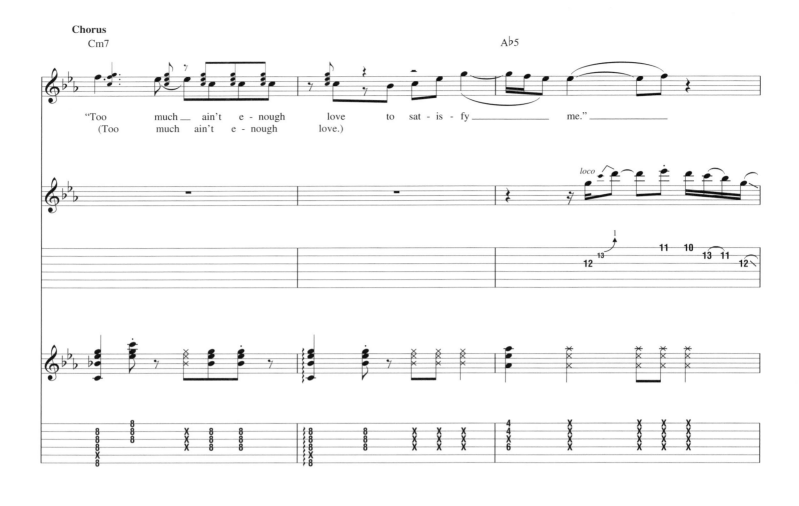

"Too much ___ ain't e - nough love to sat - is - fy _____ me." _____
(Too much ain't e - nough love.)

Yeah, _____ I said, "Too much ain't e - nough
(Too much ain't e - nough

love   to   sat - is - fy_____ me." _____   I got a burn - ing   heart,__ ba - by.
love.)

w/ Leslie effect   (Leslie effect off)

Too   much__ ain't e - nough   love   to   sat - is - fy_____ me.
(Too   much__ ain't e - nough   love.)

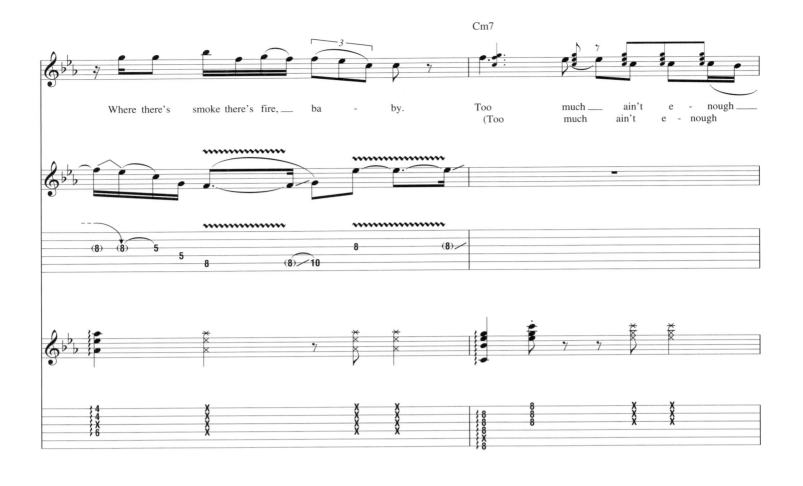

Where there's smoke there's fire, __ ba - by. Too much __ ain't e - nough __
(Too much ain't e - nough

__ love to sat - is - fy __ me. __ Hey, __ hey, __
love.)

Cm7

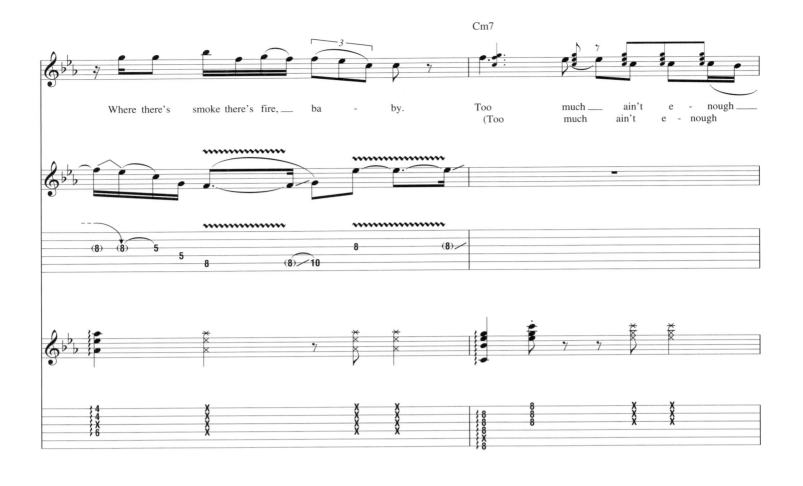

Where there's smoke there's fire, __ ba - by. Too much __ ain't e - nough __
(Too much ain't e - nough

Ab5

__ love to sat - is - fy __ me. __ Hey, __ hey, __
love.)

Guitar Solo

Gtr. 2: w/ Rhy. Fig. 1 (2 times)

Cm7

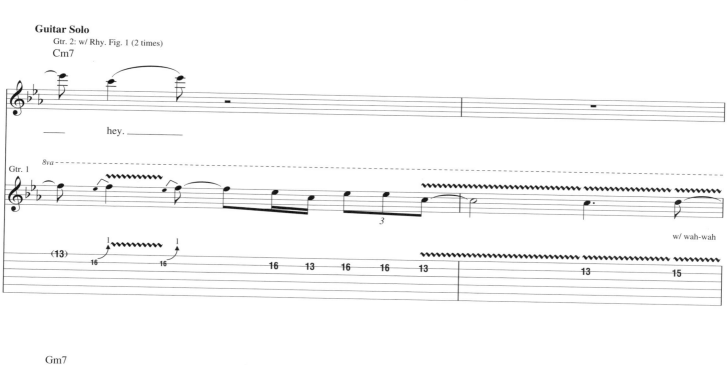

— hey. ——

Gm7

Cm7

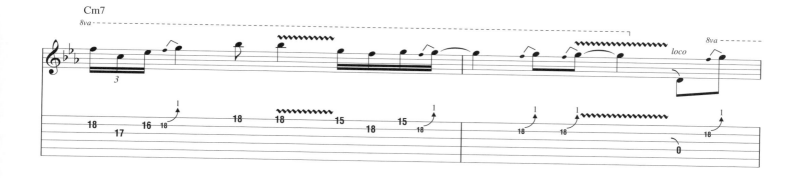

Gm7

I said, "Too, too— much ain't e-nough now, ——

Outro

Gtr. 2: w/ Rhy. Fig. 1 (7 1/2 times)

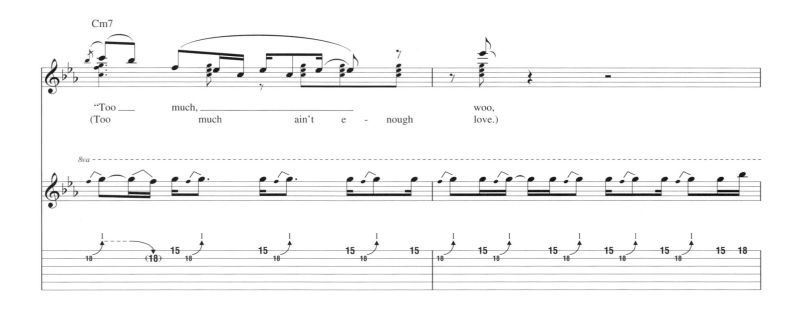

Cm7

"Too ___ much, _____ woo,
(Too much ain't e - nough love.)

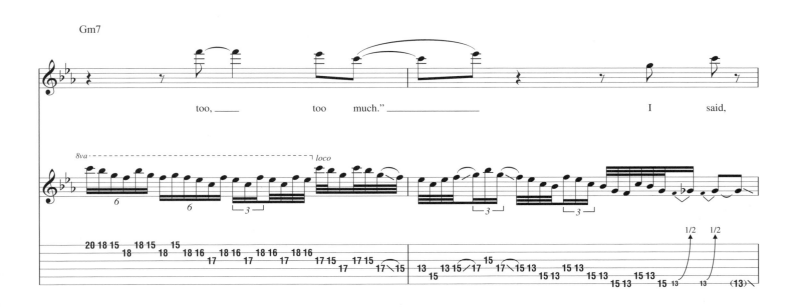

Gm7

too, ___ too much." _____ I said,

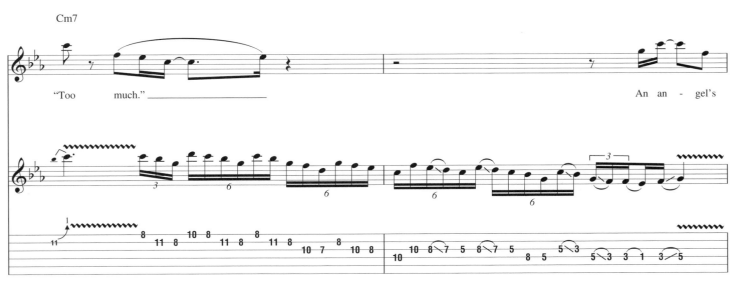

Cm7

"Too much." _____ An an - gel's

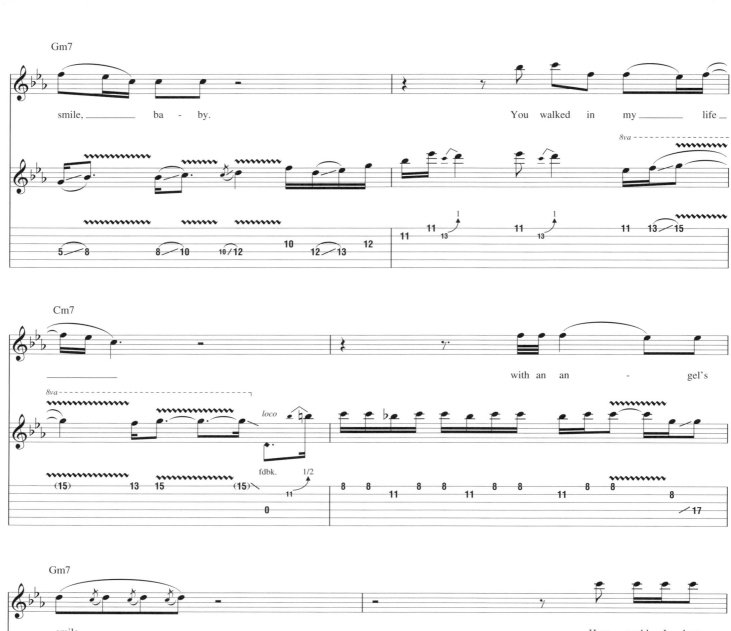

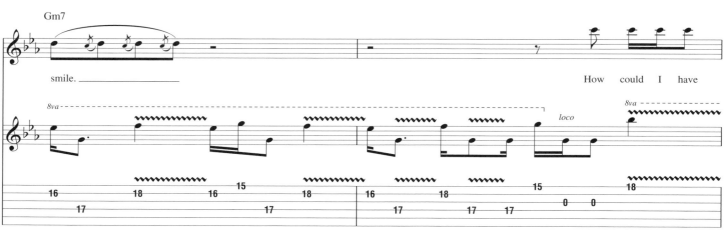

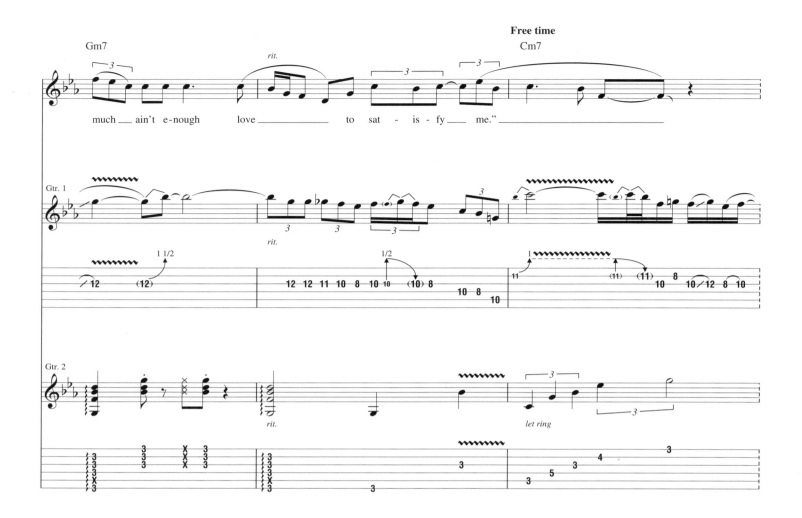

much ___ ain't e-nough   love _____ to sat - is - fy ___ me."_____

GUITAR NOTATION LEGEND

Guitar music can be notated three different ways: on a *musical staff*, in *tablature*, and in *rhythm slashes*.

RHYTHM SLASHES are written above the staff. Strum chords in the rhythm indicated. Use the chord diagrams found at the top of the first page of the transcription for the appropriate chord voicings. Round noteheads indicate single notes.

THE MUSICAL STAFF shows pitches and rhythms and is divided by bar lines into measures. Pitches are named after the first seven letters of the alphabet.

TABLATURE graphically represents the guitar fingerboard. Each horizontal line represents a string, and each number represents a fret.

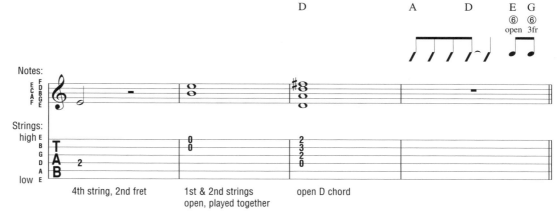

4th string, 2nd fret   1st & 2nd strings open, played together   open D chord

Definitions for Special Guitar Notation

HALF-STEP BEND: Strike the note and bend up 1/2 step.

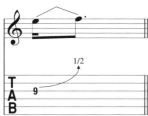

WHOLE-STEP BEND: Strike the note and bend up one step.

GRACE NOTE BEND: Strike the note and immediately bend up as indicated.

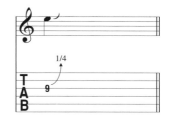

SLIGHT (MICROTONE) BEND: Strike the note and bend up 1/4 step.

BEND AND RELEASE: Strike the note and bend up as indicated, then release back to the original note. Only the first note is struck.

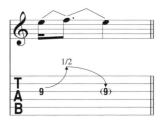

PRE-BEND: Bend the note as indicated, then strike it.

PRE-BEND AND RELEASE: Bend the note as indicated. Strike it and release the bend back to the original note.

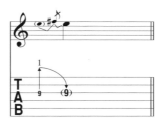

UNISON BEND: Strike the two notes simultaneously and bend the lower note up to the pitch of the higher.

VIBRATO: The string is vibrated by rapidly bending and releasing the note with the fretting hand.

WIDE VIBRATO: The pitch is varied to a greater degree by vibrating with the fretting hand.

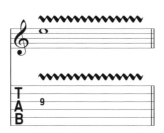

HAMMER-ON: Strike the first (lower) note with one finger, then sound the higher note (on the same string) with another finger by fretting it without picking.

PULL-OFF: Place both fingers on the notes to be sounded. Strike the first note and without picking, pull the finger off to sound the second (lower) note.

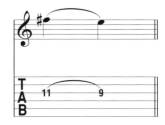

LEGATO SLIDE: Strike the first note and then slide the same fret-hand finger up or down to the second note. The second note is not struck.

SHIFT SLIDE: Same as legato slide, except the second note is struck.

TRILL: Very rapidly alternate between the notes indicated by continuously hammering on and pulling off.

TAPPING: Hammer ("tap") the fret indicated with the pick-hand index or middle finger and pull off to the note fretted by the fret hand.

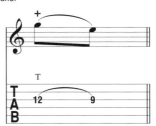

NATURAL HARMONIC: Strike the note while the fret-hand lightly touches the string directly over the fret indicated.

PINCH HARMONIC: The note is fretted normally and a harmonic is produced by adding the edge of the thumb or the tip of the index finger of the pick hand to the normal pick attack.

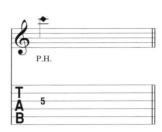

HARP HARMONIC: The note is fretted normally and a harmonic is produced by gently resting the pick hand's index finger directly above the indicated fret (in parentheses) while the pick hand's thumb or pick assists by plucking the appropriate string.

PICK SCRAPE: The edge of the pick is rubbed down (or up) the string, producing a scratchy sound.

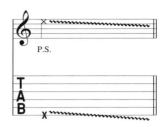

MUFFLED STRINGS: A percussive sound is produced by laying the fret hand across the string(s) without depressing, and striking them with the pick hand.

PALM MUTING: The note is partially muted by the pick hand lightly touching the string(s) just before the bridge.

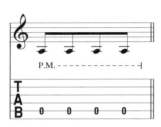

RAKE: Drag the pick across the strings indicated with a single motion.

TREMOLO PICKING: The note is picked as rapidly and continuously as possible.

ARPEGGIATE: Play the notes of the chord indicated by quickly rolling them from bottom to top.

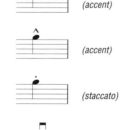

VIBRATO BAR DIVE AND RETURN: The pitch of the note or chord is dropped a specified number of steps (in rhythm), then returned to the original pitch.

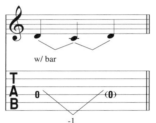

VIBRATO BAR SCOOP: Depress the bar just before striking the note, then quickly release the bar.

VIBRATO BAR DIP: Strike the note and then immediately drop a specified number of steps, then release back to the original pitch.

Additional Musical Definitions

(accent)	• Accentuate note (play it louder).	
(accent)	• Accentuate note with great intensity.	
(staccato)	• Play the note short.	
⊓	• Downstroke	
V	• Upstroke	
D.S. al Coda	• Go back to the sign (𝄋), then play until the measure marked "***To Coda***," then skip to the section labelled "**Coda**."	
D.C. al Fine	• Go back to the beginning of the song and play until the measure marked "***Fine***" (end).	

Rhy. Fig. — • Label used to recall a recurring accompaniment pattern (usually chordal).

Riff — • Label used to recall composed, melodic lines (usually single notes) which recur.

Fill — • Label used to identify a brief melodic figure which is to be inserted into the arrangement.

Rhy. Fill — • A chordal version of a Fill.

tacet — • Instrument is silent (drops out).

• Repeat measures between signs.

• When a repeated section has different endings, play the first ending only the first time and the second ending only the second time.

NOTE: Tablature numbers in parentheses mean:
1. The note is being sustained over a system (note in standard notation is tied), or
2. The note is sustained, but a new articulation (such as a hammer-on, pull-off, slide or vibrato) begins, or
3. The note is a barely audible "ghost" note (note in standard notation is also in parentheses).

RECORDED VERSIONS®
The Best Note-For-Note Transcriptions Available

ALL BOOKS INCLUDE TABLATURE

14037551	AC/DC – Backtracks	$32.99
00692015	Aerosmith – Greatest Hits	$22.95
00690178	Alice in Chains – Acoustic	$19.95
00694865	Alice in Chains – Dirt	$19.95
00690812	All American Rejects – Move Along	$19.95
00690958	Duane Allman Guitar Anthology	$24.99
00694932	Allman Brothers Band – Volume 1	$24.95
00694933	Allman Brothers Band – Volume 2	$24.95
00694934	Allman Brothers Band – Volume 3	$24.95
00690865	Atreyu – A Deathgrip on Yesterday	$19.95
00690609	Audioslave	$19.95
00690820	Avenged Sevenfold – City of Evil	$24.95
00691065	Avenged Sevenfold – Waking the Fallen	$22.99
00690503	Beach Boys – Very Best of	$19.95
00690489	Beatles – 1	$24.99
00694832	Beatles – For Acoustic Guitar	$22.99
00691014	Beatles Rock Band	$34.99
00694914	Beatles – Rubber Soul	$22.99
00694863	Beatles – Sgt. Pepper's Lonely Hearts Club Band	$22.99
00110193	Beatles – Tomorrow Never Knows	$22.99
00690110	Beatles – White Album (Book 1)	$19.95
00691043	Jeff Beck – Wired	$19.99
00692385	Chuck Berry	$19.95
00690835	Billy Talent	$19.95
00690901	Best of Black Sabbath	$19.95
00690831	blink-182 – Greatest Hits	$19.95
00690913	Boston	$19.95
00690932	Boston – Don't Look Back	$19.99
00690491	David Bowie – Best of	$19.95
00690873	Breaking Benjamin – Phobia	$19.95
00690451	Jeff Buckley – Collection	$24.95
00690957	Bullet for My Valentine – Scream Aim Fire	$22.99
00691159	The Cars – Complete Greatest Hits	$22.99
00691079	Best of Johnny Cash	$22.99
00691004	Chickenfoot	$22.99
00690590	Eric Clapton – Anthology	$29.95
00690415	Clapton Chronicles – Best of Eric Clapton	$18.95
00690936	Eric Clapton – Complete Clapton	$29.99
00690074	Eric Clapton – The Cream of Clapton	$24.95
00694869	Eric Clapton – Unplugged	$22.95
00690162	The Clash – Best of	$19.95
00101916	Eric Church – Chief	$22.99
00690828	Coheed & Cambria – Good Apollo I'm Burning Star, IV, Vol. 1: From Fear Through the Eyes of Madness	$19.95
00691188	Coldplay – Mylo Xyloto	$22.99
00690593	Coldplay – A Rush of Blood to the Head	$19.95
00690819	Creedence Clearwater Revival – Best of	$22.95
00690648	The Very Best of Jim Croce	$19.95
00690613	Crosby, Stills & Nash – Best of	$22.95
00691171	Cry of Love – Brother	$22.99
00690967	Death Cab for Cutie – Narrow Stairs	$22.99
00690289	Deep Purple – Best of	$19.99
00690784	Def Leppard – Best of	$19.95
00692240	Bo Diddley	$19.99
00690347	The Doors – Anthology	$22.95
00690348	The Doors – Essential Guitar Collection	$16.95
14041903	Bob Dylan for Guitar Tab	$19.99
00691186	Evanescence	$22.99
00690810	Fall Out Boy – From Under the Cork Tree	$19.95
00691181	Five Finger Death Punch – American Capitalist	$22.99
00690664	Fleetwood Mac – Best of	$19.95
00690870	Flyleaf	$19.95
00690931	Foo Fighters – Echoes, Silence,	

	Patience & Grace	$19.95
00690808	Foo Fighters – In Your Honor	$19.95
00691115	Foo Fighters – Wasting Light	$22.99
00690805	Robben Ford – Best of	$22.99
00694920	Free – Best of	$19.95
00691050	Glee Guitar Collection	$19.99
00690943	The Goo Goo Dolls – Greatest Hits Volume 1: The Singles	$22.95
00113073	Green Day – ¡Uno!	$21.99
00701764	Guitar Tab White Pages – Play-Along	$39.99
00694854	Buddy Guy – Damn Right, I've Got the Blues	$19.95
00690840	Ben Harper – Both Sides of the Gun	$19.95
00694798	George Harrison – Anthology	$19.95
00690841	Scott Henderson – Blues Guitar Collection	$19.95
00692930	Jimi Hendrix – Are You Experienced?	$24.95
00692931	Jimi Hendrix – Axis: Bold As Love	$22.95
00692932	Jimi Hendrix – Electric Ladyland	$24.95
00690017	Jimi Hendrix – Live at Woodstock	$24.95
00690602	Jimi Hendrix – Smash Hits	$24.99
00691152	West Coast Seattle Boy: The Jimi Hendrix Anthology	$29.99
00691332	Jimi Hendrix – Winterland (Highlights)	$22.99
00690793	John Lee Hooker Anthology	$24.99
00690692	Billy Idol – Very Best of	$19.95
00690688	Incubus – A Crow Left of the Murder	$19.95
00690790	Iron Maiden Anthology	$24.99
00690721	Jet – Get Born	$19.95
00690684	Jethro Tull – Aqualung	$19.95
00690959	John5 – Requiem	$22.95
00690814	John5 – Songs for Sanity	$19.95
00690751	John5 – Vertigo	$19.95
00690845	Eric Johnson – Bloom	$19.95
00690846	Jack Johnson and Friends – Sing-A-Longs and Lullabies for the Film Curious George	$19.95
00690271	Robert Johnson – New Transcriptions	$24.95
00699131	Janis Joplin – Best of	$19.95
00690427	Judas Priest – Best of	$22.99
00690975	Kings of Leon – Only by the Night	$22.99
00694903	Kiss – Best of	$24.95
00690355	Kiss – Destroyer	$16.95
00690834	Lamb of God – Ashes of the Wake	$19.95
00690875	Lamb of God – Sacrament	$19.95
00690823	Ray LaMontagne – Trouble	$19.95
00690679	John Lennon – Guitar Collection	$19.95
00690781	Linkin Park – Hybrid Theory	$22.95
00690743	Los Lonely Boys	$19.95
00690720	Lostprophets – Start Something	$19.95
00114563	The Lumineers	$22.99
00690955	Lynyrd Skynyrd – All-Time Greatest Hits	$19.99
00694954	Lynyrd Skynyrd – New Best of	$19.95
00690754	Marilyn Manson – Lest We Forget	$19.95
00694956	Bob Marley– Legend	$19.95
00694945	Bob Marley– Songs of Freedom	$24.95
00690657	Maroon5 – Songs About Jane	$19.95
00120080	Don McLean – Songbook	$19.95
00694951	Megadeth – Rust in Peace	$22.95
00691185	Megadeth – Th1rt3en	$22.99
00690951	Megadeth – United Abominations	$22.99
00690505	John Mellencamp – Guitar Collection	$19.95
00690646	Pat Metheny – One Quiet Night	$19.95
00690558	Pat Metheny – Trio: 99>00	$19.95
00690040	Steve Miller Band – Young Hearts	$19.95
00102591	Wes Montgomery Guitar Anthology	$24.99
00691070	Mumford & Sons – Sigh No More	$22.99
00694883	Nirvana – Nevermind	$19.95
00690026	Nirvana – Unplugged in New York	$19.95
00690807	The Offspring – Greatest Hits	$19.95
00694847	Ozzy Osbourne – Best of	$22.95
00690399	Ozzy Osbourne – Ozzman Cometh	$22.99
00690933	Best of Brad Paisley	$22.95
00690995	Brad Paisley – Play: The Guitar Album	$24.99
00694855	Pearl Jam – Ten	$22.99
00690439	A Perfect Circle – Mer De Noms	$19.95
00690499	Tom Petty – Definitive Guitar Collection	$19.95

00690428	Pink Floyd – Dark Side of the Moon	$19.95
00690789	Poison – Best of	$19.95
00693864	The Police – Best of	$19.95
00694975	Queen – Greatest Hits	$24.95
00690670	Queensryche – Very Best of	$19.95
00690878	The Raconteurs – Broken Boy Soldiers	$19.95
00694910	Rage Against the Machine	$19.95
00690055	Red Hot Chili Peppers – Blood Sugar Sex Magik	$19.95
00690584	Red Hot Chili Peppers – By the Way	$19.95
00691166	Red Hot Chili Peppers – I'm with You	$22.99
00690852	Red Hot Chili Peppers –Stadium Arcadium	$24.95
00690511	Django Reinhardt – Definitive Collection	$19.95
00690779	Relient K – MMHMM	$19.95
00690631	Rolling Stones – Guitar Anthology	$27.95
00694976	Rolling Stones – Some Girls	$22.95
00690264	The Rolling Stones – Tattoo You	$19.95
00690685	David Lee Roth – Eat 'Em and Smile	$19.95
00690942	David Lee Roth and the Songs of Van Halen	$19.95
00690031	Santana's Greatest Hits	$19.95
00690566	Scorpions – Best of	$22.95
00690604	Bob Seger – Guitar Collection	$19.95
00690803	Kenny Wayne Shepherd Band – Best of	$19.95
00690968	Shinedown – The Sound of Madness	$22.99
00690813	Slayer – Guitar Collection	$19.95
00690733	Slipknot – Vol. 3 (The Subliminal Verses)	$22.99
00120004	Steely Dan – Best of	$24.95
00694921	Steppenwolf – Best of	$22.95
00690655	Mike Stern – Best of	$19.95
00690877	Stone Sour – Come What(ever) May	$19.95
00690520	Styx Guitar Collection	$19.95
00120081	Sublime	$19.95
00120122	Sublime – 40oz. to Freedom	$19.95
00690929	Sum 41 – Underclass Hero	$19.95
00690767	Switchfoot – The Beautiful Letdown	$19.95
00690993	Taylor Swift – Fearless	$22.99
00115957	Taylor Swift – Red	$21.99
00690531	System of a Down – Toxicity	$19.95
00694824	James Taylor – Best of	$17.99
00690871	Three Days Grace – One-X	$19.95
00690683	Robin Trower – Bridge of Sighs	$19.95
00699191	U2 – Best of: 1980-1990	$19.95
00690732	U2 – Best of: 1990-2000	$19.95
00660137	Steve Vai – Passion & Warfare	$24.95
00110385	Steve Vai – The Story of Light	$22.99
00690116	Stevie Ray Vaughan – Guitar Collection	$24.95
00660058	Stevie Ray Vaughan – Lightnin' Blues 1983-1987	$24.95
00694835	Stevie Ray Vaughan – The Sky Is Crying	$22.95
00690015	Stevie Ray Vaughan – Texas Flood	$19.95
00690772	Velvet Revolver – Contraband	$22.95
00690071	Weezer (The Blue Album)	$19.95
00690966	Weezer – (Red Album)	$19.99
00690447	The Who – Best of	$24.95
00690916	The Best of Dwight Yoakam	$19.95
00691019	Neil Young – Everybody Knows This Is Nowhere	$19.99
00690905	Neil Young – Rust Never Sleeps	$19.99
00690623	Frank Zappa – Over-Nite Sensation	$22.99
00690589	ZZ Top Guitar Anthology	$24.95

Prices and availability subject to change without notice.
Some products may not be available outside the U.S.A.

0113

GUITAR *signature licks*

Signature Licks book/CD packs provide a step-by-step breakdown of "right from the record" riffs, licks, and solos so you can jam along with your favorite bands. They contain performance notes and an overview of each artist's or group's style, with note-for-note transcriptions in notes and tab. The CDs feature full-band demos at both normal and slow speeds.

AC/DC
14041352 ....$22.99

ACOUSTIC CLASSICS
00695864 ....$19.95

AEROSMITH 1973-1979
00695106 ....$22.95

AEROSMITH 1979-1998
00695219 ....$22.95

BEST OF AGGRO-METAL
00695592 ....$19.95

DUANE ALLMAN
00696042 ....$22.99

BEST OF CHET ATKINS
00695752 ....$22.95

AVENGED SEVENFOLD
00696473 ....$22.99

THE BEACH BOYS DEFINITIVE COLLECTION
00695683 ....$22.95

BEST OF THE BEATLES FOR ACOUSTIC GUITAR
00695453 ....$22.95

THE BEATLES BASS
00695283 ....$22.95

THE BEATLES FAVORITES
00695096 ....$24.95

THE BEATLES HITS
00695049 ....$24.95

JEFF BECK
00696427 ....$22.99

BEST OF GEORGE BENSON
00695418 ....$22.95

BEST OF BLACK SABBATH
00695249 ....$22.95

BLUES BREAKERS WITH JOHN MAYALL & ERIC CLAPTON
00696374 ....$22.99

BLUES/ROCK GUITAR HEROES
00696381 ....$19.99

BON JOVI
00696380 ....$22.99

KENNY BURRELL
00695830 ....$22.99

BEST OF CHARLIE CHRISTIAN
00695584 ....$22.95

BEST OF ERIC CLAPTON
00695038 ....$24.95

ERIC CLAPTON – FROM THE ALBUM UNPLUGGED
00695250 ....$24.95

BEST OF CREAM
00695251 ....$22.95

CREEDANCE CLEARWATER REVIVAL
00695924 ....$22.95

DEEP PURPLE – GREATEST HITS
00695625 ....$22.95

THE BEST OF DEF LEPPARD
00696516 ....$22.95

THE DOORS
00695373 ....$22.95

TOMMY EMMANUEL
00696409 ....$22.99

ESSENTIAL JAZZ GUITAR
00695875 ....$19.99

FAMOUS ROCK GUITAR SOLOS
00695590 ....$19.95

FLEETWOOD MAC
00696416 ....$22.99

BEST OF FOO FIGHTERS
00695481 ....$24.95

ROBBEN FORD
00695903 ....$22.95

BEST OF GRANT GREEN
00695747 ....$22.95

BEST OF GUNS N' ROSES
00695183 ....$24.95

THE BEST OF BUDDY GUY
00695186 ....$22.99

JIM HALL
00695848 ....$22.99

HARD ROCK SOLOS
00695591 ....$19.95

JIMI HENDRIX
00696560 ....$24.95

JIMI HENDRIX – VOLUME 2
00695835 ....$24.95

JOHN LEE HOOKER
00695894 ....$19.99

HOT COUNTRY GUITAR
00695580 ....$19.95

BEST OF JAZZ GUITAR
00695586 ....$24.95

ERIC JOHNSON
00699317 ....$24.95

ROBERT JOHNSON
00695264 ....$22.95

BARNEY KESSEL
00696009 ....$22.99

THE ESSENTIAL ALBERT KING
00695713 ....$22.95

B.B. KING – BLUES LEGEND
00696039 ....$22.99

B.B. KING – THE DEFINITIVE COLLECTION
00695635 ....$22.95

B.B. KING – MASTER BLUESMAN
00699923 ....$24.99

THE KINKS
00695553 ....$22.95

BEST OF KISS
00699413 ....$22.95

MARK KNOPFLER
00695178 ....$22.95

LYNYRD SKYNYRD
00695872 ....$24.95

THE BEST OF YNGWIE MALMSTEEN
00695669 ....$22.95

BEST OF PAT MARTINO
00695632 ....$24.99

MEGADETH
00696421 ....$22.99

WES MONTGOMERY
00695387 ....$24.95

BEST OF NIRVANA
00695483 ....$24.95

THE OFFSPRING
00695852 ....$24.95

VERY BEST OF OZZY OSBOURNE
00695431 ....$22.95

BRAD PAISLEY
00696379 ....$22.99

BEST OF JOE PASS
00695730 ....$22.95

JACO PASTORIUS
00695544 ....$24.95

TOM PETTY
00696021 ....$22.99

PINK FLOYD – EARLY CLASSICS
00695566 ....$22.95

THE GUITARS OF ELVIS
00696507 ....$22.95

BEST OF QUEEN
00695097 ....$24.95

BEST OF RAGE AGAINST THE MACHINE
00695480 ....$24.95

RED HOT CHILI PEPPERS
00695173 ....$22.95

RED HOT CHILI PEPPERS – GREATEST HITS
00695828 ....$24.95

BEST OF DJANGO REINHARDT
00695660 ....$24.95

BEST OF ROCK
00695884 ....$19.95

BEST OF ROCK 'N' ROLL GUITAR
00695559 ....$19.95

BEST OF ROCKABILLY GUITAR
00695785 ....$19.95

THE ROLLING STONES
00695079 ....$24.95

BEST OF DAVID LEE ROTH
00695843 ....$24.95

BEST OF JOE SATRIANI
00695216 ....$22.95

BEST OF SILVERCHAIR
00695488 ....$22.95

THE BEST OF SOUL GUITAR
00695703 ....$19.95

BEST OF SOUTHERN ROCK
00695560 ....$19.95

STEELY DAN
00696015 ....$22.99

MIKE STERN
00695800 ....$24.99

BEST OF SURF GUITAR
00695822 ....$19.95

BEST OF SYSTEM OF A DOWN
00695788 ....$22.95

ROBIN TROWER
00695950 ....$22.95

STEVE VAI
00673247 ....$22.95

STEVE VAI – ALIEN LOVE SECRETS: THE NAKED VAMPS
00695223 ....$22.95

STEVE VAI – FIRE GARDEN: THE NAKED VAMPS
00695166 ....$22.95

STEVE VAI – THE ULTRA ZONE: NAKED VAMPS
00695684 ....$22.95

STEVIE RAY VAUGHAN – 2ND ED.
00699316 ....$24.95

THE GUITAR STYLE OF STEVIE RAY VAUGHAN
00695155 ....$24.95

BEST OF THE VENTURES
00695772 ....$19.95

THE WHO – 2ND ED.
00695561 ....$22.95

JOHNNY WINTER
00695951 ....$22.99

BEST OF ZZ TOP
00695738 ....$24.95

HAL•LEONARD®
CORPORATION
7777 W. BLUEMOUND RD. P.O. BOX 13819
MILWAUKEE, WISCONSIN 53213

www.halleonard.com

COMPLETE DESCRIPTIONS AND SONGLISTS ONLINE!
Prices, contents and availability subject to change without notice.

0113